The Infinity Zone
A Transcendent Approach To Peak Performance

by

Paul Mayberry & Matthew J. Pallamary

Mystic Ink Publishing

2-19-2013

To my only begotten son,
Jacob,

As you know, travel
far enough within to
embrace the infinite,
you go far enough out
to embrace infinity.
All paths lead to...

Uncle Matt

Mystic Ink Publishing
San Diego, CA
www.mysticinkpublishing.com

ISBN 10: 0615696910 (sc)
ISBN 13: 978-0615696911 (sc)
Printed in the United States of America
North Charleston, South Carolina

This book is printed on acid-free paper made from 30% post-consumer waste recycled material.

Library of Congress Control Number: 2012949222

Book Jacket and Page Design: Matthew J. Pallamary / San Diego CA
Cover Photograph: Pleiades Star Cluster courtesy of NASA / Hubble Space Telescope
Author's Photographs: Matthew J. Pallamary -- Gibbs Photo / Malibu CA
Paul Mayberry -- Paul Mayberry

DEDICATION

This book is dedicated to Colleen Kennedy, Patricia Hill, Howard Mayberry, Eric Hart, Rudolf Steiner, Charles M. Schulz, and Ray Bradbury.

CONTENTS

ACKNOWLEDGEMENTS

The authors wish to acknowledge the support of Jack Broudy, Lace Chess, Rose Snowing, Rob Gubala, Kim Gubala, Margaux Hession, The Santa Barbara Writer's Conference, The Southern California Writer's Conference, Grail Sports, and Rudolf Steiner, whose work inspired The Infinity Zone.

FOREWORD

One of my earliest thoughts about infinity had to do with the feeling of extending out to the edge of space and wondering what was on the other side. Whenever I came to an end, I found a new beginning. Contemplating a mobius strip or imagining my arm extending to one side, I envisioned connecting with the other side as if in a globe; bridging a gap with the unknown.

Playing ball in school playgrounds honed my skills and understanding of infinity, helping me to excel at tennis. A great tennis facility lay between home and school. I hung out at the backboard there to be alone with my thoughts while hitting endless balls and became one of the top juniors in Southern California.

Around the age of twelve, I was introduced to tai chi by a teacher who used the back yard of our family's preschool to give classes. My father and I became obsessed with a hybrid style of the basic tai chi ball movement we called the figure 8. Effortless movement was the ideal.

My father used to write one-liners on large adding machine paper at a podium where his gyrations punctuated the verse he was writing. He usually wrote in a paradoxical form that expressed some aspect of polarity, like "Chicken sooth is meta zen".

Infusing movement and thought became a preoccupation that fueled my interest in research and teaching. Eastern tai chi practices brought me to a whole new level that culminated in the discovery of

Rudolf Steiner. Steiner's works related to projective geometry, spatial dynamics, and the etheric realm. I incorporated anything that I thought might improve my play.

In my early twenties I attended workshop lectures at the Rudolf Steiner College in Fair Oaks Sacramento. In a flash I realized that the figure 8 movement could be the basis of a movement system that I could teach in a new way. Until that moment, I felt unable to encompass what tennis pros were really doing.

I taught lessons, revealing the figure 8 as a symbol of all the elements of a stroke, stressing the 45 degree angle as the ideal hitting point and midpoint of a focused rotation with the center in perfect relationship to the centrifugal power at the periphery.

Everything changed when I met a successful tennis pro named Jack Broudy. When I tested some ideas on Jack's students, he was impressed enough to become a business partner and co-creator. Together we developed the 8board and inspired our student knights in the quest for perfection, symbolized by the Grail.

The real work was done on the practice court, with King Jack and Merlin looking deeper into the mystery of infinity for depth and insight as we mastered our craft over many years. We both coached in the south of France for 15 years on a property with a real castle, working with a group of students from the age of five to the present day.

All of them are phenomenal players.

I am in awe of meeting Matthew Pallamary after reading an article he wrote on the theory and evolution of consciousness, sensing instant karma when it all came together.

I am truly grateful for our collaboration and experience, and I am excited about the future with a book like this to inspire a new generation of players who are ready to learn the secrets of The Infinity Zone.

Paul Mayberry   May 23, 2012

INTRODUCTION

"I think that the leaf of a tree, the meanest insect on which we trample, are in themselves arguments more conclusive than any which can be adduced that some vast intellect animates Infinity."

-- Percy Bysshe Shelley

"The 'infinity' is spread all over!! The 'infinity' and the 'boundless one' (God) both meet at a point. "

-- Atharva Veda

Albert Einstein said, "Everything is energy and that's all there is to it. Match the frequency of the reality you want and you cannot help but get that reality. It can be no other way. This is not philosophy. This is physics."

Physics is a natural science that involves the study of matter and its motion through space-time along with its related concepts of energy and force. More broadly, it is the general analysis of nature, conducted in order to understand how the universe behaves.

The Infinity Zone is a phenomena that occurs at the nexus of perfect form and motion that when utilized properly, can bring balance, power, and control to a number of physical and mental activities on multiple levels.

Based on the form and motion of the Figure 8, the Infinity Zone applies its dynamics back and forth through the inner spectrum of cognition across the boundaries of thought and matter and back again, from the mental to the physical; to the depths of infinity inside of us to the boundless infinity without.

In order to navigate the physical world our senses take in a multitude of stimuli, much of it through the eyes and ears. What our senses take in, our minds process continuously, reinterpreting the incoming data from moment to moment, instantaneously making adjustments to the shifting environment. By regulating our breathing, heartbeat, and blood pressure, as well as other unconscious physiological functions, our body's natural intelligence strives for balance; especially when it is involved in intense physical activity that requires great coordination, like sports or dancing.

This rapid exchange between inner subjectivity and outer objectivity is an infinity pattern between external stimulus and inner interpretation. The continuous volley and serve of stimulus and response moves back and forth in the same manner as a tennis match, only this match is played at very high speed with multiple volleys.

A tennis player who has mastered the Infinity Zone not only has the poised "inner game of tennis" where matches are won; they also control the outer world through the movement of their bodies through the Infinity Zone, making them superior players.

Not only are they doing a rapid subjective objective dance; the two sides of their brain are also communicating on many levels, instantaneously sending masses of information volleying back and forth across the "net" of the corpus callosum, the central area in the fissure of the brain that facilitates communication between both sides. When the motion of their body comes into harmony with their whole being in the form of the figure 8, their body, mind, and emotion are balanced, operating at peak power and efficiency -- in the Infinity Zone.

The laws of physics that the Infinity Zone follows are prevalent throughout the natural world as well as through the geometry of projective space which has *more* points than Euclidean space where every point is determined by the three dimensions of length, width, and height. Because of their prevalence, these forms and functions are brought to light through the study of Sacred Geometry which shows through the universal language of mathematics, the perfection of natural form and motion.

The next geometric progression is time, the fourth dimension, which follows the same rules of geometry. Here the three dimensions become active, moving from static to dynamic, into the vector of time.

Universal principles of perfect form and motion are apparent in the Infinity Zone. This elegant peak of power and efficiency through form and movement is ubiquitous throughout nature, art, music, and sports.

Once practiced and understood, the Infinity Zone is realized as a higher state of consciousness that can be applied to achieve transcendent peak performance.

Its power is universal.

ONE

SACRED GEOMETRY

"Infinite is a meaningless word: except – it states / The mind is capable of performing / an endless process of addition."

-- Louis Zukofsky

"I'm only a four-dimensional creature. Haven't got a clue how to visualise infinity. Even Einstein hadn't. I know because I asked him."

-- Patrick Moore

Sacred geometry is used in the planning and construction of religious structures such as churches, temples, mosques, religious monuments, altars, and tabernacles as well as sacred spaces such as sacred groves, village greens and holy wells, and in the creation of religious art.

Cathédrale Notre-Dame de Chartres

Chartres North Rose Window

In sacred geometry, symbolic and sacred meanings are ascribed to certain geometric shapes and geometric proportions. In the ancient world certain numbers had symbolic meaning aside from their ordinary use for counting or calculating. Plane figures, polygons, triangles, squares, hexagons, and so forth were related to numbers in the same manner as the number three is to the triangle. Because they were visual, they carried more emotional value than the numbers themselves.

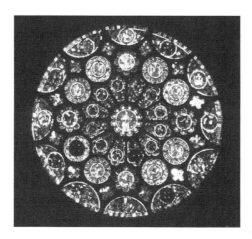

Chartres South Rose Window

The belief that God created the universe according to a geometric plan has ancient origins. Plutarch attributed the belief to Plato, writing "Plato said God geometrizes continually".

The study of sacred geometry has its roots in the study of nature and the mathematical principles at work there. Many natural forms can be related to geometry, such as the chambered nautilus, which grows at a constant rate. Its shell forms a logarithmic spiral to accommodate that growth without changing shape.

Honeybees construct hexagonal cells to hold their honey and the bumblebee compound eye is formed of a large number of individual hexagonal units called ommatidia. These and other correspondences in nature provide further proof of the cosmic significance of geometric forms, all of which can be explained through natural principles.

Honeycomb

Bumblebee eye showing individual ommatidia

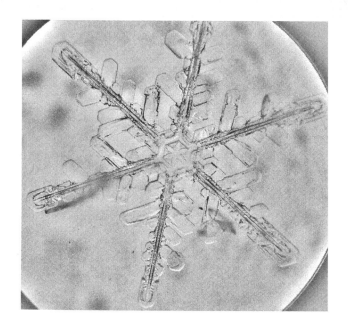

Snowflake

Passion Flower

The golden ratio, geometric ratios, and geometric figures were often employed in the design of Egyptian, ancient Indian, Greek and Roman architecture. Medieval European cathedrals also incorporated symbolic geometry. Indian and Himalayan spiritual communities constructed temples and fortifications on design plans based on the mandala.

Mandala

In philosophy, especially that of Aristotle, the golden mean is the desirable middle between two extremes, one of excess and the other of deficiency. As an example courage, a virtue, if taken to excess would manifest as recklessness, and if found to be deficient as cowardice.

To the Greek mentality it was an attribute of beauty. Both ancients and moderns realized a close association in mathematics between beauty and truth. The poet John Keats, in his *Ode on a Grecian Urn*, put it this way: "Beauty is truth, truth beauty, -- that is all ye know on earth, and all ye need to know."

The Greeks believed there to be three ingredients to beauty: symmetry, proportion, and harmony. This triad of principles infused their life. They were attuned to beauty as an object of love and something to be imitated and reproduced in their lives, architecture, education, and politics. They judged life by this mentality.

In Chinese philosophy, a similar concept, Doctrine of the Mean, was propounded by Confucius; Buddhist philosophy also includes the concept of the middle way.

The Golden Ratio lies at the core of sacred geometry. Also known as the Golden Cut, the Golden Rectangle, The Divine Proportion, and other names, the Golden Mean, like PI π (**3.14**) is another of those strange numbers that we seldom question and often take for granted. This magical, infinite number (**1.618**) is represented by the Greek letter PHI ϕ. Different from PI, the golden mean goes unnoticed in our everyday life in such things as buildings, plants, and living creatures, yet we find these things strangely pleasing to the eye.

An ancient mathematician by the name of Fibonacci discovered that if you start with the numbers **0** and **1** and add them together you get a new number -- in this case **1**. If you add the last number and the new number together, you get another new number, **2**. If you keep doing this, you end up with a long list of unique numbers known as the Fibonacci Series.

0, 1 — Added together gives a new number **1**.
0, 1, 1 -- Add the last two numbers and new number is **2**.
0, 1, 1, 2 -- Add the last two numbers and the new number is **3**.
0, 1, 1, 2, 3 -- Add the last two numbers and the new number is **5**.
0,1,1,2,3,5 -- The additions grow into a series of unique numbers.
0,1,1,2,3,5,8,13,21,34,55,89,144, 233,377 to infinity.

Starting from zero, if you take any two SEQUENTIAL numbers and calculate the ratio between them, an interesting pattern emerges.

1,0	Ratio	=	1	to	0	=	0
1,1	Ratio	=	1	to	1	=	1
2,1	Ratio	=	2	to	1	=	2
3,2	Ratio	=	3	to	2	=	1.5
5,3	Ratio	=	5	to	3	=	1.6666
8,5	Ratio	=	8	to	5	=	1.6
13,8	Ratio	=	13	to	8	=	1.625
21,13	Ratio	=	21	to	13	=	1.61538
34,21	Ratio	=	34	to	21	=	1.61538
55,34	Ratio	=	55	to	34	=	1.61764
89,55	Ratio	=	89	to	55	=	1.6181
144,89	Ratio	=	144	to	89	=	1.6179

If you continue in this manner the decimal figure will revolve around the magic number **1.618** because it is an infinite number.

Here is an example of how the golden mean occurs in nature. The diagram below is made up of squares, but the overall image is a rectangle that has the magic ratio of **1.618**. The curved lines within each of the squares are quarter circles, but as a whole they look like the cross section of a sea shell. This is in fact the same as the growth rate of the beautiful Nautilus Sea Shell - i.e. **1.618**.

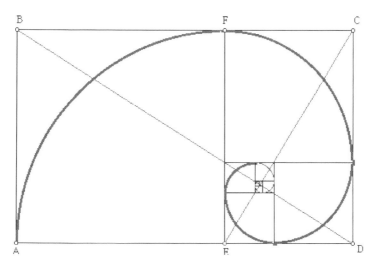

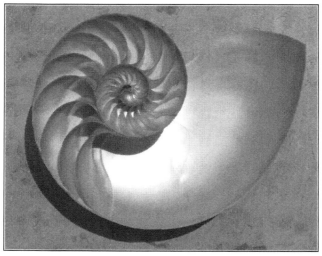

Cutaway of a Chambered Nautilus

Another interesting phenomenon of the Fibonacci sequence and the golden mean within nature is the sunflower. If you count the spirals, there are **55** with either **34** or **89** on either side going in a counter clockwise direction, which is a Fibonacci sequence. If a Fibonacci number is divided by its immediate predecessor in the sequence, the quotient approximates the golden mean.

Fibonacci Spirals in a Sunflower

Other examples abound on both microcosmic and macrocosmic scales.

Fractals in a Romanesco broccoli

A low pressure area shows a logarithmic spiral pattern.

The arms of spiral galaxies often have the shape of logarithmic spirals, like those shown here in the Whirlpool Galaxy.

Contemporary use of the term *sacred geometry* describes assertions of a mathematical order to the intrinsic nature of the universe. Scientists see the same geometric and mathematical patterns arising from natural principles.

Aside from the golden spiral, among the most prevalent traditional geometric forms ascribed to sacred geometry are:

The Sine Wave

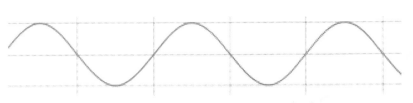

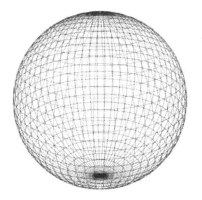

The Sphere

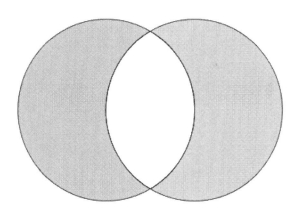

The Vesica Piscis

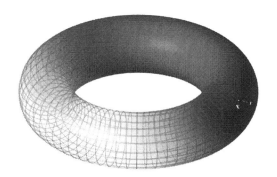

The Torus

THE 5 PLATONIC SOLIDS

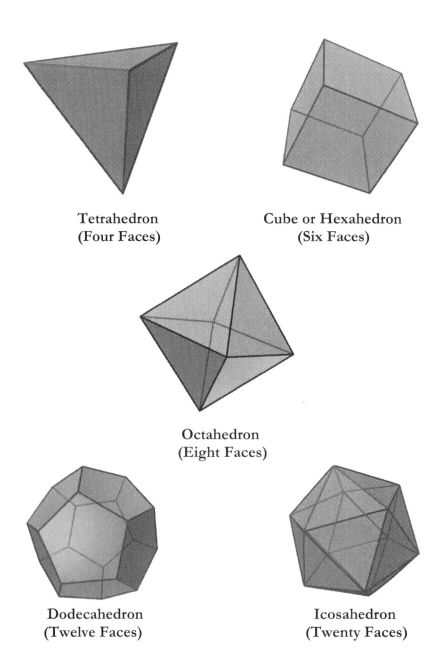

Tetrahedron
(Four Faces)

Cube or Hexahedron
(Six Faces)

Octahedron
(Eight Faces)

Dodecahedron
(Twelve Faces)

Icosahedron
(Twenty Faces)

Star Tetrahedron

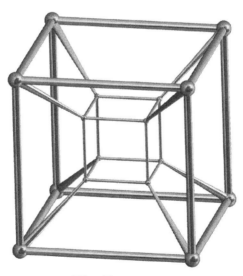

The <u>Tesseract</u>
(4-dimensional cube)

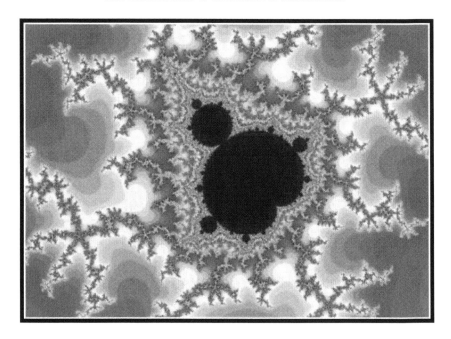

Fractals

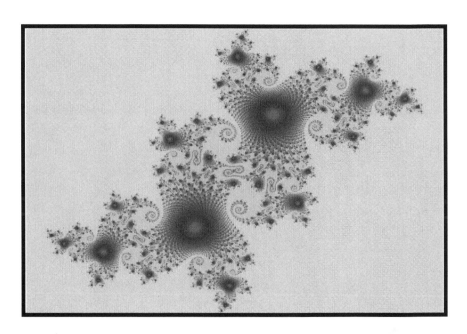

Many of the sacred geometric principles of the human body and ancient architecture have been compiled into the well known Vitruvian Man drawing by Leonardo Da Vinci, based on the much older writings of the Roman architect Vitruvius.

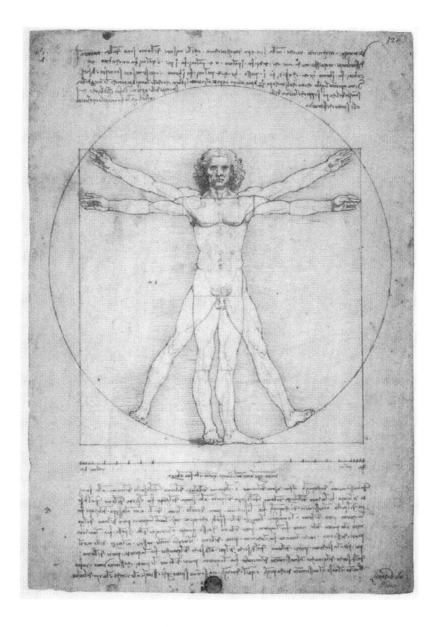

The Vitruvian Man

TWO

THE TEMPLE OF MAN

"What is man in nature? Nothing in relation to the infinite, all in relation to nothing, a mean between nothing and everything"

-- Blaise Pascal

"The interior of our skulls contains a portal to infinity."

— Grant Morrison

The geometric principles of the human body and ancient architecture were recorded long before the Roman architect Vitruvius and Da Vinci came up with their now famous drawing.

Ancient wisdom from many cultures tells us that our body is our temple. One of the most profound, densely packed storehouses of wisdom on our planet is contained in the temple of Amun-Mut-Khonsu in Egypt.

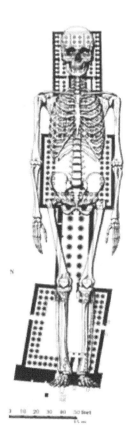

The Temple of Anthropocosmic Man

This Temple of Anthropocosmic Man at Luxor is a masterpiece of art, science, and spirituality laid out in an elegant structure that is architecturally rendered to exhibit within its design and artwork the same proportions as the proportions of Man, as well as the mathematical and geometrical structure of the Cosmos and its locale within human consciousness. Pharaonic Consciousness not only recognized Man as the center of the Universe, it could formally equate it as well.

In his smaller work, "The Temple *in* Man", that distills the massive two volume set "The Temple *of* Man", R. A. Schwaller de Lubicz shares his observations of the temple. "…the canon proportions of the profile and the head, and of the head in relation to the body, are present. Here the Golden Number comes to our aid. It controls all vegetable and animal growth…"

He continues to write: "The outline of a human skeleton—traced according to anthropometrical methods and very carefully constructed, bone by bone—was superimposed on the general plan of the temple. The head (full face for the skeleton) is located exactly in the sanctuaries of the covered temple; the sanctuary of the barque of Amun is in the oral cavity; the clavicles are marked by walls; the chest is located in the first hypostyle of the covered temple and ends with the temple's platform. The abdomen is represented by the peristyle court, and the pubis is located exactly at the door separating

27

this peristyle from the colonnade of Amun.

This marvelous colonnade is, in fact, dedicated to the femurs, the thighs; the knees are at the site of the gate in front of which sit the two colossi, marking the entrance to this colonnade. The tibias are in the court of Ramses, framed by the colossi, whose legs (tibias) are particularly pronounced. The little toe of our skeleton falls exactly at the northwest angle of the pylon. One might be tempted to think this skeleton had been constructed to be superimposed on the temple. But any skeleton, as long as it is harmonious (like the one represented here) can be projected thus on the plan of the temple and will coincide with it. Moreover, all the proportions of the skeleton may be checked against the actual measurements of the temple.

For my report, it was necessary to have recourse to the Egyptian canon; I have in this regard devoted a chapter to a subject that has never been dealt with until now—the importance the Ancients accorded the crown of the skull (cava).

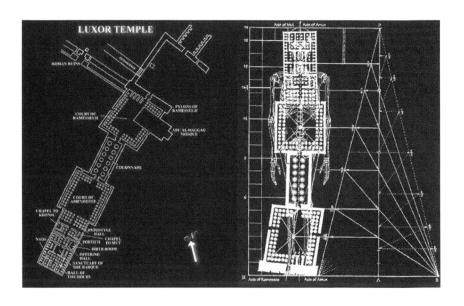

Mathematical Proportions of the Luxor Temple

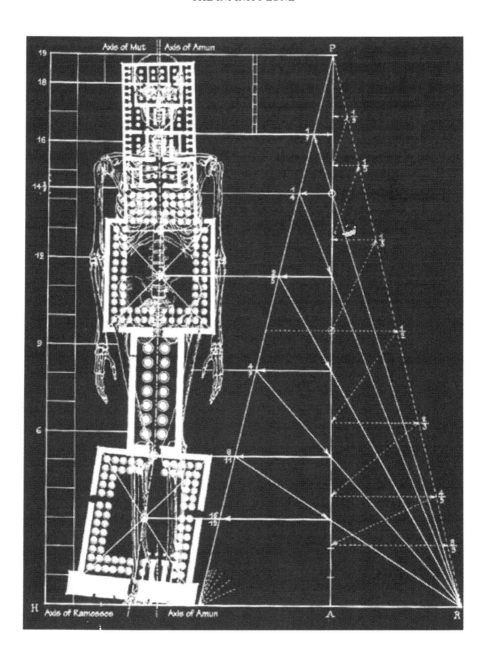

Close-up of Temple Proportions

This crown of the skull, marked off in Egyptian figuration by a headband, a diadem, a headdress or crown—is a veritable revelation with regard to psycho-spiritual knowledge of the Ancients.

This is made clear by the placement of the principal organs of the Intellect and of all the control mechanisms of life in the various sanctuaries, whose figurations, texts, and architecture specify their purpose.

The Temple of Luxor is indisputably devoted to the Human Microcosm. This consecration is not merely a simple attribution: the entire temple becomes a book explaining the secret functions of the organs and nerve centers."

The human body is phi-designed as the golden section template seen throughout our whole human form ratios, proving that humans, like the macrocosm of the planets and stars, and the microcosm of atomic and subatomic particles were all created using the PHI design.

The first example of the golden ratio in the average human body is when the distance between the navel and the foot is taken as **1** unit, the height of a human being is equivalent to **1.618.**

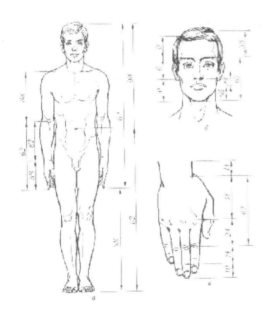

Human Body Proportions

Some other golden proportions in the average human body are:

- The distance between the finger tip and the elbow and the distance between the wrist and the elbow.

- The distance between the shoulder line and the top of the head and the head length.

- The distance between the navel and the top of the head and the distance between the shoulder line and the top of the head.

- The distance between the navel and knee and the distance between the knee and the end of the foot.

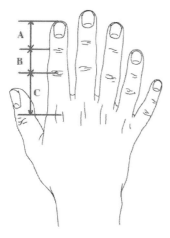

Our fingers have three sections. The proportion of the first two to the full length of the finger gives the golden ratio (with the exception of the thumbs. The proportion of the middle finger to the little finger is also a golden ratio.

We have two hands, and the fingers on them consist of three sections. There are five fingers on each hand. Only eight of these are articulated according to the golden number: **2, 3, 5,** and **8** fit the Fibonacci numbers.

Likewise, there are several golden ratios in the human face. The total width of the two front teeth in the upper jaw over their height gives a golden ratio. The width of the first tooth from the centre to the second tooth also yields the golden ratio of **1.618**. These are the ideal proportions that a dentist may consider.

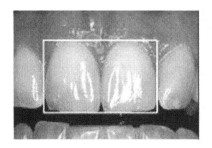 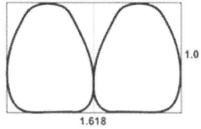

Golden Ratio Between Front Teeth Width and Height

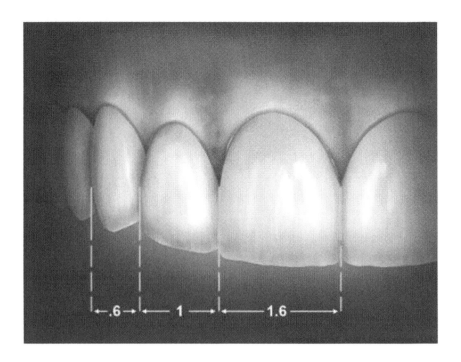

Golden Ration Between First and Second Tooth

Some other golden ratios in the human face are:

- Length of the face to the width of the face.

- The distance between the lips and where the eyebrows meet and the length of the nose.

- The length of the face and the distance between the tip of jaw and where the eyebrows meet.

- The length of the mouth and the width of the nose.

- The width of the nose and the distance between the nostrils.

- The distance between the pupils and the distance between the eyebrows.

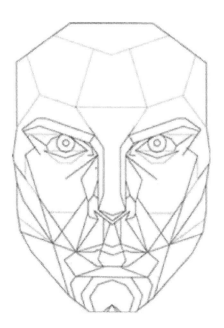

Golden Ratios in the Human Face

On a molecular level, the DNA molecule, which is the program for all life, is based on the golden mean which measures **34** angstroms long by **21** angstroms wide for each full cycle of its double helix spiral. **34** and **21** are numbers in the Fibonacci series and their ratio, **1.6190476** closely approximates phi, **1.6180339**.

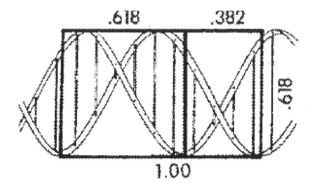

Golden Mean in DNA

Dr. Stephen Marquardt has studied human beauty for years in his practice of oral and maxillofacial surgery. Marquardt performed cross-cultural surveys on beauty and found that all groups had the same perceptions of facial beauty. The more symmetric the face, the more it is considered beautiful. He also analyzed the human face from ancient times to modern day. His research showed that beauty is not only related to phi, it can be defined for both genders and for all races, cultures, and eras, giving credence to the ancients who recognized the association in mathematics between beauty and truth.

Mathematical Association Between Beauty and Truth

Our consciousness resides at the center of our awareness which is a magical Infinity Zone where inner meets outer, spirit meets matter, and the thoughts of our infinite inner reality interact with the infinity of "external" reality.

Every physical attribute of a human being is geometrically definable in three dimensions according to the cosmic laws of sacred geometry and the divine proportion.

The cosmic laws of sacred geometry also apply to the fourth dimension, which is time. The interplay of the dimensions of time and space through consciousness are made evident by applying geometric functions to the science of projective geometry.

THREE

THE FOURTH DIMENSION

"No finite point has meaning without an infinite reference point"

-- Jean-Paul Sartre

"The infinite is in the finite of every instant"

-- Zen Proverb

In the three dimensional reality that we inhabit, everything that evolves must have a beginning where all that manifests comes into being. This nexus is defined as the point of origin where the intangible becomes tangible and the first duality that defines our existence comes into play. This infinity point is the basis for our dualistic three dimensional world view that is played out endlessly in the way that we perceive it.

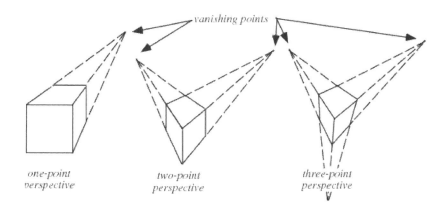

Points of Origin Represented by Vanishing Points

Spirit-matter, subject-object, positive-negative, yin-yang, male-female, day-night, sleeping-waking, and life-death are a small sampling of the dual archetype that provides the basis for life. It manifests in the inhale-exhale of our lungs, the beating of our hearts, the ticking of our clocks, our music in the primal beats of a drum, and the notes which would not be differentiated without the spaces between them.

Yin Yang Symbol

Musical Note Duration for 4/4 Quarter Notes

Two is also the basis for our world wide computerization and it's web of information, based on the simple binary notation of ones and zeroes. The permutations of duality are endless, but to understand its origins we need to get to the point, where it all began.

.

Point

A point has no size and can only be imagined. It fixes a location in space and has a dimension equal to zero. If you take a point and move it from its original location to another location, this moving point creates a line which constitutes the first dimension, known as length.

Line

This movement is a manifestation of energy, which is the essence of consciousness.

When we move a line which has no thickness from its original location to another location, it leaves the first dimension and becomes a plane which has two dimensions, length and width.

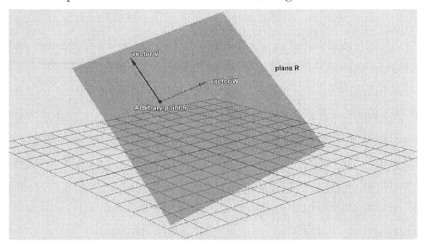

Plane

When we move a plane, it leaves two dimensions and creates a solid body with three dimensions, length, width, and height. If each of these dimensional shifts cover the same distance, the result is a cube, the basic representation of three dimensional reality represented by 2^2, known as two to the second power, or two cubed.

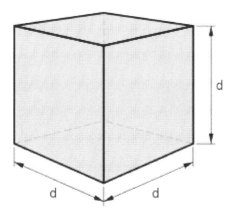

Three Dimensional Cube

When you move a three dimensional body in space, it remains a three dimensional body and does not leave the third dimension.

If you imagine yourself without any dimensions, you would be formless. Zero dimension is the point, the first dimension indicating energetic movement is the line, the second dimension is the surface, and the third dimension is the solid body. If you imagine yourself as a being who can only move along the first dimension of a straight line, all you would see is points, not your own dimensionality, because when we attempt to draw something within a line, points are the only option.

A two-dimensional being moving through a plane would encounter lines and thus distinguish one-dimensional beings. A three-dimensional being, such as a cube, would encounter planes and perceive two dimensional beings. Human beings however, can perceive three-dimensions.

A one-dimensional being can perceive only points, a two-dimensional being only one dimension, and a three-dimensional being only two dimensions. By the logic of this progression it becomes apparent that the perception of each dimension necessitates being one dimension above it. Therefore human beings who can delineate external beings in three dimensions and manipulate three-dimensional spaces must be four dimensional beings. Just as a cube can perceive only two dimensions and not its own third dimension, it is also true that human beings cannot perceive the fourth dimension in which we live.

The movement of the point to make the line, the line to the plane, and the plane to the solid, all take time, making time synonymous with movement. We perceive the energetic movement of our three dimensional bodies through space as time. How long does it take to get from point A to point B?

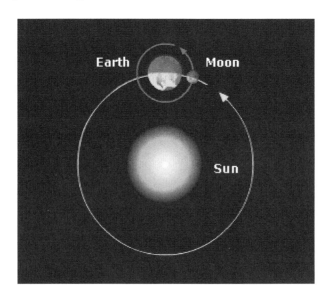

Orbits of the Earth and the Moon

Our whole concept of time and our calendar is based on physical movement, specifically by counting the number of identical cyclical movements that a particular time measurement corresponds to. It takes three hundred and sixty five and a quarter days for the earth to circle the sun in a solar year, one month for the moon to circle the earth, a day of twenty four hours for the earth to complete a rotation on its axis, sixty minutes to make up an hour, and sixty seconds to make up a minute.

Our materialistic world view has us locked in to time perception based on the movement of physical bodies through space, but what of the source of the expansion and its point of origin that make up the other unseen, formless half of the formula?

This formless half of the formula comes from inside of us where the seat of consciousness resides, perched between subject and object in the Infinity Zone, where the evolution of consciousness takes place.

The Infinity Zone
(Seat of Consciousness)

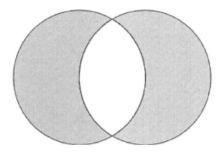

Subject   **Object**
(Inner Perception) (Outer Perception)

A shift in our perceptions brings a shift in how we live in and perceive the world from our present fourth dimensional existence that perceives a three dimensional world, to fifth dimensional existence where we perceive the fourth dimension, transcending time and duality.

New discoveries in quantum physics lay the ground for this by proving that matter is more empty space than solidity. In the terms of Einstein's famous $E=MC^2$, matter is another form of energy, and energy is the essence of consciousness. The fundamental nature of this paradox tells us that positive and negative are extremes. It is the energy between them that matters. That is where the action is and where we exist within ourselves; at the threshold of subject and object, in the center, mid-point of our duality. When we transcend the poles, we become centered in the Infinity Zone and rise above the opposition of forces to embrace the energy that they manifest.

When the mid-point rises above the baseline, its transcendence creates a triad, trinity, or triangle.

Infinity Point

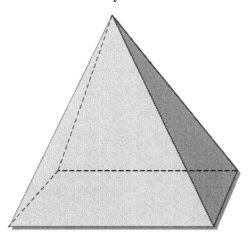

Pyramid Symbolizing Transcendence

The three dimensional representation of a triangle with four sides creates a pyramid, one of the greatest enigmas known to mankind. The square base of a pyramid represents the four dimensions and the four directions of the physical world and rises up pointing toward the heavens in a diminishing apex that represents an infinity point where matter ends and spirit begins.

Similar to the example of the pyramid, the laws of geometry are self evident when moving from three dimensional space to fourth dimensional time through the study of projective geometry.

Euclidean geometry describes shapes as they are. Their properties of length, angles, and parallelism are unchanged by rigid motions.

Projective geometry describes objects as they appear. Lengths, angles, and parallelism become distorted when we look at objects from this perspective which provides a mathematical model for how images of the 3 dimensional world are formed.

Projective geometry is the branch of mathematics that deals with the relationships between geometric figures and the images, or mappings that come from projecting them onto another surface.

Common examples are the shadows cast by opaque objects and motion pictures displayed on a screen.

As shown below, the eye is connected to points on the landscape of the horizontal reality plane, *RP*, by sight lines. The intersection of these lines with the vertical picture plane, *PP* generates the drawing, projecting the reality plane onto the picture plane, hence the name *projective* geometry.

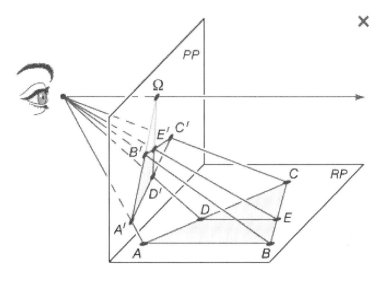

Projective Geometry

Counter space is the space where subtle forces not amenable to ordinary measurement work. Instead of having its ideal elements in a plane at infinity it has them in a "point at infinity". They are lines and planes rather than lines and points as in ordinary space, and are known as *counter space infinity*. A plane incident with it is said to be an *ideal plane* or *plane at infinity* in counter space. It only appears for a different, peripheral kind of consciousness that experiences such a point as infinite inwardness in contrast to normal consciousness that experiences infinite outwardness.

In counter space terms, the Infinity Zone is known as a linkage; an element that belongs to both Euclidian and counter space at once, such as a point or plane. If a cube is linked to both spaces at once, and is moved upward away from the inner infinitude, it will obey the metrics of both spaces. The diagram below shows what happens as it moves. The smaller version obeys space and stays the same size and shape in space, while the bigger version obeys the counter space metric.

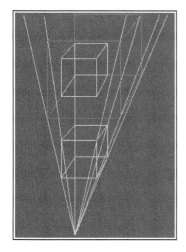

The counter space, or inner infinity, is shown as a point at the bottom. Lines drawn from it through the vertices of the cube stay on these lines, obeying its metric properties, illustrated by the smaller cube while the smaller spatial cube stays the same spatially. This seems natural with our ordinary consciousness, but for counter space consciousness the other is most natural and the projected cube appears to be getting bigger.

Counter Space

The geometric difference between the two cubes is referred to as *strain,* analogous to the use of that term in engineering where it is the percentage deformation in size, like when a rubber band is stretched. The rubber band responds to the strain by exerting a force referred to as *stress.*

The central principles here are:

- Objects may be linked to both spaces at once.

- When they are, strain arises when they move because the metrics are conflicting.

- Stress arises as a result of the strain.

Stress is not a geometric concept. We move from geometry to physics when we consider it. The major stress free movement or transformation is rotation about an axis through the counter space infinity. This focal "power point" axis that is the core of stress free movement and transformation is the Infinity Zone.

FOUR

THE INFINITY ZONE

"If any philosopher had been asked for a definition of infinity, he might have produced some unintelligible rigmarole, but he would certainly not have been able to give a definition that had any meaning at all."

-- Bertrand Russell

"There is a fifth dimension, beyond that which is known to man. It is a dimension as vast as space and as timeless as infinity. It is the middle ground between light and shadow, between science and superstition."

-- Rod Serling

When a pendulum swings down it moves at its greatest speed when it passes the middle point and it goes slower and slower as it rises on the other side until it reverses its movement. The greatest amount of energy is at the center, as opposed to the extremes where the power is the weakest. The greatest power in our solar system lies in the sun that resides at its center. If you look at a terrestrial energy manifestation like a hurricane, one of the most powerful forces of nature, it revolves around the eye of the storm, which is its calmest place; its center of power.

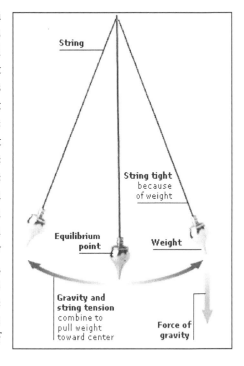

Solar System

In our dualistic world view, we tend to focus on the extremes, falsely believing them to be the places of maximum power, but the greatest power always resides in understanding that it is not the polarities that deserve our attention, it is the energy in between; the Infinity Zone.

The mathematical symbol that represents the three dimensional form and fourth dimensional motion is a sideways figure 8 - ∞. The central point of the infinity symbol where transition occurs represents the center of the Infinity Zone where the greatest power lies.

It is no accident that tremendous power has been attributed to the number 8. It has great meaning and significance throughout history and cultures the world over. In numerology it is considered the most powerful of all numbers.

The number **8** is the base figure of the octal number system and has been the axis around which the number systems evolved across the globe. The most commonly used decimal system can be chronologically traced back to the octal system, adding more substance to the belief that the number **8** is the number of regeneration and new life.

The properties, qualities, and beliefs around the number **8** are seemingly endless. Its multitude of attributes have been culled to give examples from the many realms that it influences.

In mathematics:

- **8** is a composite number, its proper divisors being **1, 2,** and **4**. It is twice **4** or four times **2**. Eight is a power of two, being 2^3.

- The Prime Factors of **8=2x2x2**.

- **8** is the base of the octal number system, which is mostly used with computers. In octal, one digit represents **3** bits. In modern computers, a byte is a grouping of eight bits, also called an octet.

- **8** is the largest cube in the Fibonacci Sequence, being **3** plus **5**. The next Fibonacci number is **13**. **8** is the only positive Fibonacci number, aside from **1**, that is a perfect cube.

- the center. If we know that the greatest power is in the middle, we transcend the opposites,

- The maximal number of regions into which a plane can be divided by **3** circles = **8**

- **8** is the maximal number of regions into which space can be divided by **3** Spheres.

- A polygon with eight sides is an octagon.

- Figurate numbers representing octagons (including eight) are called octagonal numbers. A polyhedron with eight faces is an octahedron. A cuboctahedron has as faces six equal squares and eight equal regular triangles.

- A Truncated Tetrahedron is an Archimedean Solid with **8** Faces. It has four triangles and four hexagons.

- The Cube is a Platonic Solid with **8** Vertices.

- Sphenic numbers always have exactly eight divisors.

- A figure **8** is the common name of a geometric shape, often used in the context of sports, such as skating. Figure-eight turns of a rope or cable around a cleat, pin, or bitt are used to belay something.

In Physics:

- In nuclear physics **8** is the second magic number.

- In particle physics the eightfold way is used to classify sub-atomic particles.

In Astronomy:

- As of 2006, in our Solar System, eight of the bodies orbiting the Sun are considered to be planets.

In Chemistry:

- The atomic number of oxygen.

- The number of allotropes of carbon.

- The most stable allotrope of a sulphur molecule is made of eight sulphur atoms arranged in a rhombic form.

- The maximum number of electrons that can occupy a valence shell.

In Biology:

- All spiders, and more generally all arachnids, have eight legs. Orb-weaver spiders of the cosmopolitan family Areneidae have eight similar eyes.

- The octopus and its cephalopod relatives in genus Argonauta have eight arms (tentacles).

In General:

- Timothy Leary identified a hierarchy of eight levels of consciousness.

- In human adult dentition there are eight teeth in each quadrant. The eighth tooth is the so-called wisdom tooth.

- There are eight cervical nerves on each side in man and most mammals.

- In chess, each side has eight pawns and the board is made of **64** squares arranged in an eight by eight lattice. The eight queens puzzle is a challenge to arrange eight queens on the board so that none can capture any of the others.

According to the Richard Phillips web site:

- Eight is the third number that stays the same when written upside down.

- Scorpions have eight legs.

- According to Indian mythology, the Earth is supported on the backs of eight white elephants.

- Before the rise of Christianity, there were eight days in the Greek and Roman weeks.

- Many words beginning *oct-* are related to the number eight. An octopus has eight arms and an octet is a group of eight musicians.

- An octagon is a figure with eight sides and an octahedron has eight faces.

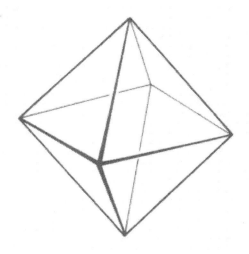

Eight Triangular Faces on an Octahedron

1	x	8	+	1	=	9
12	x	8	+	2	=	98
123	x	8	+	3	=	987
1 234	x	8	+	4	=	9 876
12 345	x	8	+	5	=	98 765
123 456	x	8	+	6	=	987 654
1 234 567	x	8	+	7	=	9 876 543

123 456 789 x 8 + 9 = 987 654 321

Mathematical Magic with the Number Eight

According to the Riding the Beast web site, the number 8 has the following properties:

Symbolism:

- Number of the perfection, the infinity. In mathematics the symbol of the infinity is represented by a **8** laid down.

- Symbol of the cosmic Christ.

- Number figuring the immutable eternity or the self-destruction. It represents also the final point of the manifestation.

- In China, **8** expresses the totality of the universe.

- Number of the balance and of the cosmic order, according to the Egyptians.

- Number expressing matter, it is also the symbol of the incarnation in matter which becomes itself creative and autonomous, governing its own laws.

- The number eight corresponds to the New Testament, according to Ambroise.

- It is the symbol of the new Life, the final Resurrection and the anticipated Resurrection that is the baptism.

- According to Clement of Alexandria, the Christ places under the sign of **8** the one he made to be born again.

- Represent the totality and the coherence of the creation in evolution. In China, it expresses the totality of the universe.

- Represent the earth, not in its surface but in its volume, since **8** is the first cubic number.

- The Pythagoreans have made the number **8** the symbol of love and friendship, prudence and thinking. They called it the Great "Tetrachtys".

- In Babylon, Egypt, and Arabia, it was the number of the duplication devoted to the sun, from where the solar disc is decorated with a cross of eight arms.

- The number **8** means multiplicity for the Japanese.

- A favorable number, associated to the prosperity.

- It is the number of the restful day, after the 7th day of the creation.

General:

- The number eight governs the life of man: at **8** months the baby teeth appear; at **8** years, he loses them; at **2** x **8** years, it is puberty; and he becomes impotent at **8** x **8** years.

- Eight is the total number of Chakras of the man, counting the seven in correlation with the physical body, plus an additional working in the etheric body. This eighth Chakra is known as "the Chakra of the Soul" or "the Star Chakra", located approximately **7** to **10** centimeters above the Crown Chakra.

- The eight great gods of the Vedas: Surya, Candra, Agni, Yama, Varuna, Indra, Vâyu and Kubera.

- The eight "trigrams" of "Fou-Hi" Chinese philosopher.

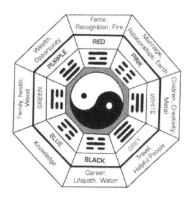

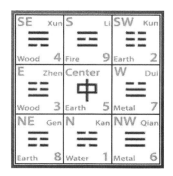

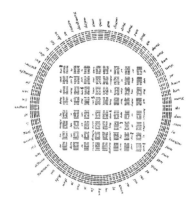

Chinese Trigrams

54

- The eight parts of the way which leads to the nirvana, according to the Buddhist doctrines: the faith, the right judgement, the right language, a right and pure action, a right profession, the application of the spirit to all the precepts of the law, the right memory and the right meditation.

- The Buddhists count eight symbols of long life of which one of them is the infinite node being rolled up and withdrawn on itself.

- There are eight degrees of Buddhist monks or "Aryas" and the highest is named "Arhat".

- According to a Buddhist legend, Buddha's ashes were separated in eight parts.

- The lotus is represented symbolically with **8** petals and according to yogis, it is on a lotus with **8** petals that the "Mêru" mount is erected which, symbolically, represents the center and the axis of the world.

- Yoga counts eight training courses: Yama, the restriction; Niyama, religious observances; Asana, the posture; Pranayama, the control of the breathing; Praty-ahara, the restriction of senses; Dharana, the concentration; Dhyana, the contemplation and Samadhi, the ecstasy.

From the Mystical Numbers web site:

- Eight symbolizes the ability to make decisions.

- Eight symbolizes abundance and power.

- The Pythagoreans called the number eight "Ogdoad" and considered it the "little holy number".

- In China eight is homonym for prosperity. When pronounced it sounds much like the word "prosper".

- A double eight, as in **88**, is said to bring double joy.

- The eighth day of the Chinese New Year is the day for the annual gathering of all the gods in Heaven.

- In the Tarot, eight is the card for Justice or Strength.

- The stop sign has eight sides.

- It takes eight minutes for the sun's light to reach the earth.

- In Ancient Rome the eighth day was an important day to a newborn child. If the newborn lived to the eighth day the child was worth special attention. On this day the baby was rubbed with salt for protection against evil spirits.

- Hinduism - The Star of Lakshmi. Lakshmi is the Hindu goddess of Wealth. The Star of Lakshmi is the eight pointed star made up of two squares. The points symbolize the eight kinds of wealth provided by Lakshmi.

Culturally, from a mythological perspective, **Apollo 8**, the second crewed mission in the American Apollo space program was the first human spaceflight to leave Earth's orbit; the first to be captured by and escape from the gravitational field of another celestial body; and the first crewed voyage to return to Earth from another celestial body—Earth's Moon.

Those milestones are the most significant and literally the farthest reaching, most powerful accomplishments of modern man.

Whether thought of as coincidence or not, the number 8 held a powerful collective meaning as Apollo 8 became the first spacecraft to break free from the gravitational field of the Earth and be captured by and escape from the gravitational field of another celestial body.

Apollo 8 Logo

According to The Numbers and Their Meanings blogspot, the number 8:

Resolves dualities, expansion, dissolution, dimension of the timeless, good and bad, right and wrong, day and night, ability to see and relate to eternal dimensions, balance between forces, connects spirit and matter, developing confidence to follow a vision, breaks down barriers to transformation, reality, courage.

All of these qualities transcend duality and bridge realities, manifesting tremendous power by resolving the paradox of opposites in a transformation from two into one.

Because the number **8** symbolizes power, it is shifted ninety degrees to symbolize infinity, ∞ which refers to something *without any limit*. It is a concept relevant in a number of fields, predominantly mathematics and physics. Having a recognizable history in these disciplines reaching back into the time of ancient greek civilization, the term in the english language derives from Latin *infinitas*, which is translated as "unboundedness".

In mathematics, "infinity" is often treated as a number, but it is not the same kind of number as the real numbers. In number systems incorporating infinitesimals, the reciprocal of an infinitesimal is an infinite number, i.e. a number greater than any real number.

The mathematical symbol for infinity is called the lemniscate. The infinity sign was devised in **1655** by mathematician John Wallis, and named lemniscus (latin, ribbon) by mathematician Bernoulli about forty years later. The lemniscate is patterned after the device known as a mobius (named after a nineteenth century mathematician Mobius) strip.

Mobius Strip

A mobius strip is a strip of paper that is twisted and attached at the ends, forming an 'endless' two dimensional surface. The religious aspect of the infinity symbol predates its mathematical origins. Similar symbols have been found in Tibetan rock carvings; and the ouroboros, or infinity snake, is often depicted in this shape. In the tarot, it represents the balance of forces and is often associated with the magician card.

Ancient cultures had numerous ideas about the nature of infinity. The ancient Indians and Greeks, unable to codify infinity in terms of a formalized mathematical system approached it as a philosophical concept.

FIVE

THE INFINITY ZONE IN NATURE

"To see a world in a grain of sand and heaven in a wild flower
Hold infinity in the palms of your hand and eternity in an hour."

-- William Blake

"By confronting us with irreducible mysteries that stretch our
daily vision to include infinity, nature opens an inviting and
guiding path toward a spiritual life."

-- Thomas More

The Infinity Zone is prevalent throughout the natural world, providing stunning examples of its perfect form and motion as it bridges the third and fourth dimensions. It is evident in the grace, beauty, and elegance in the lives of the tiniest insects up through the highest mammals.

Most insects possess wings during part of their life cycles. Insect wings are large folds in the exoskeleton composed of two sheets of cuticle permeated with stiff supportive veins powered by two sets of muscles that independently drive the upstroke and downstroke of the wing movement. The frequency of wing beats ranges from 4 beats per second in butterflies to nearly 1000 beats per second in gnats.

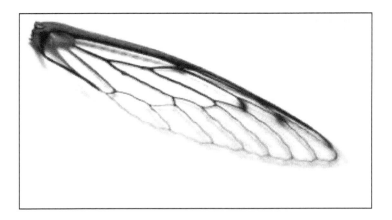

Insect Wing

Insect wings not only move up and down, they move forward and backward in an ellipse or figure eight pattern.

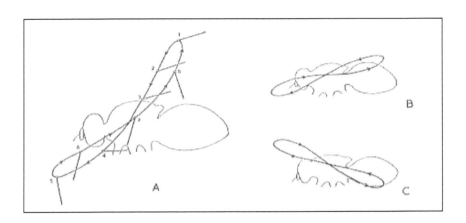

Insect Wing Movements

Given their shape, speed, and stroke pattern, it has never been clearly understood how insect wings can generate enough lift to sustain flight. Scientists have discovered that insects generate a vortex, or spiral air motion along the leading edge of their wings. This vortex flows out toward the wing tip widening spirals. The whirling cylinder of air above the insect provides the extra lift that makes flight possible.

A butterfly actually has four wings; two forewings and two hindwings. When the butterfly flexes its thorax muscles to fly it forms a figure-eight pattern.

Blue Morpho Butterfly

Insects are the only invertebrates that possess this capability that enables them to exist in great numbers of environmental situations. They are much more diverse than other invertebrates, with approximately one million species described.

The typical insect wing is a superbly designed flying tool consisting of a thin membrane reinforced throughout with numerous veins resulting in a functional compromise between weight and strength. The anterior portion of the wing is stiffened with a heavy costal vein, then the wing becomes thinner and more flexible toward the trailing edge. This structure is capable of a strong sculling action analogous to fanning air into a fire. Using a flat board for this is ineffective, but a small piece of rug held stiff on one margin, or a flexible piece of cardboard is more effective.

Insects with two pairs of wings frequently join the anterior and posterior wings by means of hooks and grooves to create a single sculling unit. Insects that don't have their wings joined overcome the problem of air turbulence by beating the front and rear pairs alternately.

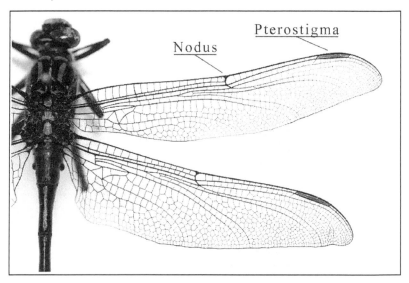

Dragonfly Wings

Wing movement in insects is complex, consisting of elevation and depression, fore and aft movement, pronation and supination, (twisting) and changes in shape by folding and buckling. The wingtips describe a figure-8 pattern. Many insects can hover or fly backward by changing the angle of the figure-8. Some of the best fliers can fly sideways or rotate about the head or tail by employing unequal wing movement. The wing movement of insects is so efficient that it produces a polarized flow of air from front to rear during 85 per cent of the wingbeat cycle.

The bumblebee is a four-winged insect. Its wings swivel and flap, knocking into each other, producing a buzzing sound. Despite the small area of its wings, the swirling vortices produced when the wings collide provide additional lift.

Bumblebee

Bumblebees, like their honeybee cousins, feed on pollen and nectar. A bumblebee often identifies where a food source is by flying in a figure-8 pattern around it.

Honeybee workers perform a series of movements, often referred to as the "waggle dance," to teach other workers the location of food sources more than 150 meters from the hive. Scout bees fly from the colony in search of pollen and nectar. If successful in finding good supplies of food, the scouts return to the hive and "dance" on the honeycomb.

Honeybee

The honeybee first walks straight ahead, vigorously shaking its abdomen and producing a buzzing sound with the beat of its wings. The distance and speed of this movement communicates the distance of the foraging site to the others. Communicating direction becomes more complex as the dancing bee aligns her body in the direction of the food, relative to the sun. The entire dance pattern is a figure-eight, with the bee repeating the straight portion of the movement each time it circles to the center again.

Moving up in the animal kingdom from pollinating insects to birds, the hummingbird utilizes a similar flying strategy. In order to hover, a hummingbird's wings move back and forth horizontally, drawing a narrow, elegant figure eight in the air with each full stroke which is continuous like a Mobius strip, the symbol of infinity.

Hummingbird

The key to a hummingbird's flight is in its wing patterns. Generally, birds flap their wings up and down. The hummingbird flies by oscillating its wings forward and backward rapidly in a figure-eight.

Seventy-five percent of its lift is produced during the down stroke. The figure-eight pattern is similar to a swimmer doing figure eights in the water to remain afloat. Imagine making a figure-8 with your arms 80 times within one second. This isn't humanly possible, but it is possible for a hummingbird.

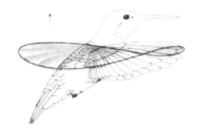

Hummingbirds are incredible athletes reaching their maximum velocity within seconds after take off without using their legs for momentum. It's all in the wings. Depending on the size of the hummingbird, their wing beat ranges anywhere from 10 up to 200 times per second. One of the largest hummingbirds known as the Giant Hummingbird has a wing beat rate of 10-15 beats per second, while the smallest Bee Hummingbird beats its wings at 80 beats per second. Common North American species like the Ruby-throat Hummingbird averages 53 beats per second.

The pectoral muscles are the most important muscles of a hummingbird. Supracoracoideus muscles, the largest part of the pectorals, known as the elevator muscles, help raise the wings during take off and flight. These muscles are attached to the sternum. Together they make up about 25-35% of a hummingbirds overall weight, over 10% more than other birds.

A hummingbird's heart is a relatively large organ in comparison to a hummingbird's body weight. It makes up 1.75% to 2.5% of the hummingbird's total weight, making the hummingbird's heart relatively the largest heart in the animal kingdom. A hummingbird's heart beats about 250 beats per minute at rest and about 1,260 beats per minute while flying.

From a metaphysical perspective it is interesting to note that relatively speaking, the largest heart in the animal kingdom is the one that perfectly masters the power of the infinity zone.

In the marine realm, dolphins and fish move swiftly through the water by moving their tails in a rapid figure 8 motion, creating figure 8 vortices that move them along. It's the fastest, most efficient means of mobility in the realm of water.

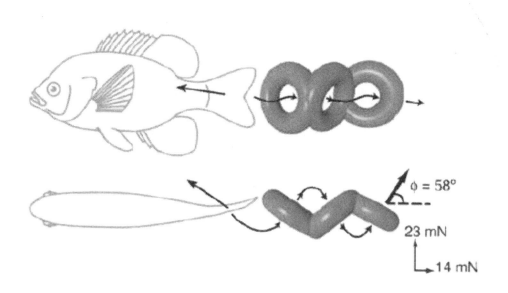

$\phi = 58°$

23 mN

14 mN

Movement of Fish Tails

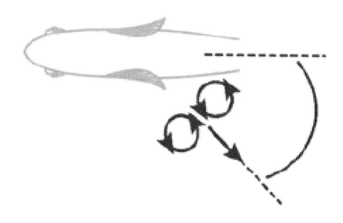

When a cheetah sprints, it leaps with both forelegs forward, propelling itself until its front legs meet the back legs, at which point the back legs pick up on the sprint, blasting forward like a second stage booster, once more propelling its forelegs forward, all in a fluid and dynamic figure 8, giving it the maximum speed and peak performance possible in the most fluid, efficient, and elegant manner.

Sprinting Cheetah

The gallop of a horse, dogs, wolves, and other canines, and the bounding of cheetahs and other cats all move in efficient figure 8 movements that demonstrate peak performance that is in harmony with natural forces, giving greater, more precise control. Its natural beauty is self apparent.

SIX

THE INFINITY ZONE IN ART AND MUSIC

"Music fills the infinite between two souls"

-- Rabindranath Tagore

"Music is well said to be the speech of angels; in fact, nothing among the utterances allowed to man is felt to be so divine. It brings us near to the infinite."

-- Thomas Carlyle

Art and music reflect the inner life of man, appealing to his innate sense of beauty, inspired by the natural world around him. The geometries present in these disciplines are an integral part of what we perceive as beauty.

When we flow from three dimensional form to four dimensional movement and back again, we dance between inner and outer infinities in a dynamic rapid-fire exchange of subject and object. We recognize the grace of these relationships in nature and mimic its perfection visually in the static arts of painting and photography, and in the dynamic arts of film, dance, and other forms of movement, as well as the auditory bliss of divinely inspired music.

In ancient Greece, mathematical disciplines introduced in childhood combined gymnastics and music until age **17** or **18**, emphasizing gymnastics until the age of **20**. This training was designed to stabilize the equilibrium of the soul, viewed by Plato as straddling the upper Intelligible realm and the lower Sensible realm so the individual could recognize the symmetry and harmony common to both music and bodily movement. The intention was for the equilibrium established in the souls of individuals to be reflected in the harmony of the State.

In Egyptian belly dancing a figure **8** with hips is comprised of two different isolations, the hip slide and the twist. The belly dance reverse figure 8 move is called the Turkish figure **8** which requires the dancers to pull in towards the center.

Contra dance choreography specifies the dance formation known as the *figures* and the sequence of those figures in a dance. The figures usually repeat a consistent pattern aligned with the phrasing of the music. A figure is a pattern of movement that typically takes eight counts, although figures with four or sixteen counts are common. Each dance is a collection of figures assembled to allow the dancers to progress along the set.

Typical contra dance choreography comprises four parts, each 16 counts or **8** measures long. Most contra dance tunes have two parts, each **8** measures long, each fitting one part of the dance. A contra dance is typically **64** counts with a **32**-measure tune.

To get the most effective rim shot on a snare drum, the swing of the arm and the wrist flex upward in a bend, making the first half of a figure **8**, then come down, snapping the wrist in a whip like action in the second half, catching the rim and the head of the drum simultaneously, resulting in a powerful "crack" sound.

Choreographed movements in time and space like those associated with dance and music multiply and enhance the activity of the infinity zone of the left and right brain informational volleys and serves across the "net" of the corpus callosum; a flat bundle of neural fibers that connects the left and right hemispheres of the brain.

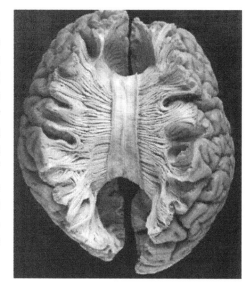

Corpus Callosum

This process is highly active in drumming as described in "The Healing Power of the Drum" by Robert Lawrence Friedman.

"One of the most powerful aspects of drumming and the reason that people have done it since the beginning of being human is that it changes people's consciousness. Through rhythmic repetition of ritual sounds, the body, brain and the nervous system are energized and transformed. When a group of people play a rhythm for an extended period of time, their brain waves become entrained to the rhythm and they have a shared brain wave state. The longer the drumming goes on, the more powerful the entrainment becomes. It's really the oldest holy communion. All of the oldest known religious rites used drumming as part of the shared religious experience.

It is interesting to look at these ancient drumming practices from the perspective of the latest scientific research into the functioning of the brain. Using electroencephalographs, scientists can measure the number of energy waves per second pulsing through the brain. A system of classifying states of consciousness according to the frequencies of these waves was created.

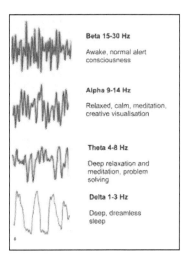

Beta 15-30 Hz

Awake, normal alert consciousness

Alpha 9-14 Hz

Relaxed, calm, meditation, creative visualisation

Theta 4-8 Hz

Deep relaxation and meditation, problem solving

Delta 1-3 Hz

Deep, dreamless sleep

Brain Waves

Normal outwardly focused attention generates beta waves which vibrate from 14 to 40 cycles per second. When awareness shifts to an internal focus, our brain slows down into the more rhythmical waves of alpha, vibrating at 7-14 waves per second. Alpha is defined by relaxation and centering. Dropping down to 4-7 cycles per second the brain enters the theta state in which there is an interfacing of conscious and unconscious processes, producing hypnologic dream-like imagery at the threshold of sleep.

Theta is the course of sudden mystical insights and creative solutions to complex situations and is marked by physical and emotional healing. People with a preponderance of theta brainwaves are also able to learn and process much more information than normal. Without some form of intensive training it is hard to stay awake in theta--one slips quickly down into delta. This is the slowest brainwave frequency, 1-5 cycles per second, the state of unconsciousness or deep sleep.

The brain is divided into two hemispheres that are basically split in their control of the thinking process. The right brain functions as the creative, visual, aural and emotional center. The left brain is the rational, logical, analytical and verbal administrator. Generally, either the right or left brain dominates in cycles lasting from 30 minutes to 3 hours. While one hemisphere is dominant, the memories, skills, and information of

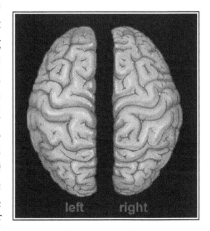

left   right

the other hemisphere are far less available, residing in a subconscious or unconscious realm. Not only do the right and left brain operate in different modes, they also usually operate in different brain wave rhythms. The right brain may be generating alpha waves while the left brain is in the beta state. Or both can be generating the same type of brain waves, but remain out of sync with each other. But in states of intense creativity, deep meditation or under the influence of rhythmic sound, both hemispheres may become entrained to the same rhythm. This state of unified whole brain functioning is called hemispheric synchronization or the awakened mind."

Music appeals to our sense of beauty through sound that expresses infinity in time. We appreciate the beauty of music when the musician has mastered the use of octaves, sound, timing, silences, and the universal mathematical laws inherent in its structure. Its appeal is universal.

Pythagoras is often credited for discovering that an oscillating string stopped halfway along its length produces an octave relative to the string's fundamental, while a ratio of 2:3 produces a perfect fifth and 3:4 produces a perfect fourth, but the Chinese already had instruments that were thousands of years older, such as the Guqin, that also feature these tonal scales.

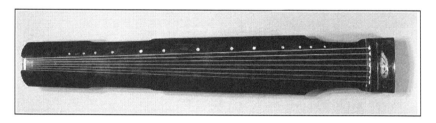

Gugin

Pythagoreans believed that these harmonic ratios gave music powers of healing which could "harmonize" an out-of-balance body. This belief has been revived in modern times.

In Music:

- A note played for one-eighth the duration of a whole note is called an eighth note, or quaver.

- An octave, the interval between two notes with the same letter name (where one has double the frequency of the other), is so called because there are eight notes between the two on a standard major or minor diatonic scale, including the notes themselves, without chromatic deviation. The ecclesiastical modes are ascending diatonic musical scales of eight notes or tones comprising an octave.

- There are eight notes in the octatonic scale.

- There are eight musicians in a double quartet or an octet. Both terms may also refer to a musical composition for eight voices or instruments.

An octave is the interval in music between two notes where the higher note has twice the frequency of the lower. On a piano keyboard this corresponds to an interval of eight white notes, for example, the notes C D E F G A B C.

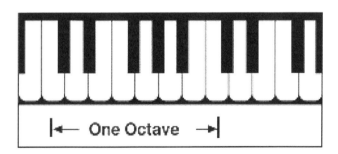

A musical scale sounds incomplete unless you play all eight notes, which is why there are eight notes rather than seven in an octave.

The term *octave* belongs to Western music, but the musical interval occurs in music around the world.

Harmony is the use of simultaneous pitches, tones, notes, or chords. The study of harmony involves chords and their construction and chord progressions and the principles of connection that govern them. Harmony is said to refer to the "vertical" aspect of music as distinguished from melodic line, or "horizontal" aspect. Counterpoint refers to the interweaving of melodic lines, and polyphony refers to the relationship of separate independent voices. They are sometimes distinguished from harmony.

In popular and jazz harmony, chords are named by their root plus various terms and characters indicating their qualities. In many types of music, notably baroque, romantic, modern, and jazz, chords are augmented with "tensions".

A tension is an additional chord member that creates a dissonant interval in relation to the bass. Typically, in the classical Common practice period a dissonant chord (chord with tension) will "resolve" to a consonant chord. Harmonization sounds pleasant to the ear when there is a balance between the consonant and dissonant sounds. It occurs when there is a balance between "tense" and "relaxed" moments.

This concept is known as relaxed tension, which is the central point where energy is mastered in balance. Every high level tennis player, drummer, dancer, or athlete knows the effortlessness of this center of power and control.

Musica universalis, known as universal music, or music of the spheres, is an ancient philosophical concept that regards proportions in the movements of celestial bodies; the Sun, Moon, and planets as a form of musica, the Medieval Latin name for music. This 'music' is not usually thought to be literally audible, but a harmonic and/or mathematical and/or religious concept. The idea appealed to musical thinkers until the end of the Renaissance, influencing scholars of many kinds, including humanists.

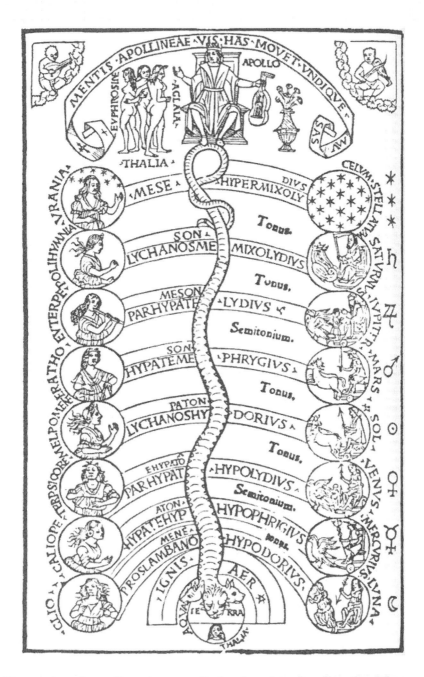

Engraving from Renaissance Italy showing Apollo, the Muses, the planetary spheres, and musical ratios.

The Music of the Spheres incorporates the metaphysical principle that mathematical relationships express qualities or 'tones' of energy that manifest in numbers, visual angles, shapes and sounds, all connected within a pattern of proportion. Pythagoras first identified that the pitch of a musical note is in proportion to the length of the string that produces it, and that intervals between harmonious sound frequencies form simple numerical ratios.

In a theory known as the Harmony of the Spheres, Pythagoras proposed that the Sun, Moon and planets all emit their own unique hum known as orbital resonance, based on their orbital revolution, and that the quality of life on Earth reflects the tenor of celestial sounds which are physically imperceptible to the human ear. Subsequently, Plato described astronomy and music as "twinned" studies of sensual recognition: astronomy for the eyes and music for the ears, both requiring knowledge of numerical proportions.

Later philosophers kept the close association between astronomy, optics, music, and astrology, including Ptolemy, who wrote influential texts on these topics. Alkindi, in the 9th century, developed Ptolemy's ideas in *De Aspectibus* which explores many points of relevance to astrology and the use of planetary aspects.

In the 17th century, Johannes Kepler influenced by arguments in Ptolemy's *Tetrabiblos, Optics and Harmonica,* compiled his Harmonices Mundi, 'Harmony of the World', that presented his own analysis of optical perceptions, geometrical shapes, musical consonances, and planetary harmonies. According to Kepler, the connection between sacred geometry, cosmology, astrology, harmonics, and music is through *musica universalis*. Kepler regarded this text as the most important work of his career, and the fifth part, concerning the role of planetary harmony in creation, the crown of it. His premise was that, as an integral part of Universal Law, mathematical harmony is the key that binds all parts together: one theoretical proposition from his work introduced the minor planetary aspects and harmonics into astrology; another introduced Kepler's third law of planetary motion into astronomy.

The three branches of the Medieval concept of musica were presented by Boethius in his book *De Musica*:

- *musica mundana*; sometimes referred to as *musica universalis*

- *musica humana*; the internal music of the human body

- *musica quae in quibusdam constituta est instrumentis;* sounds made by singers and instrumentalists

According to Max Heindel's Rosicrucian writings, the heavenly "music of the spheres" is heard in the *Region of Concrete Thought*, the lower region of the mental plane, which is an ocean of harmony. It is also referred to in Esoteric Christianity as the place where the state of consciousness known as the "Second Heaven" occurs.

When this universal order is embraced, the infinite realms that we see outside of ourselves are reflected in the infinite realms inside of ourselves, and the polar aspects of the infinity zone come into resonance, making us one in universal harmony.

This is what it means to be empowered.

SEVEN

THE INFINITY ZONE IN SPORTS

"Chair or no chair: a binary relation. But the vicissitudes of moving the body around are infinite. You never know what a person in a chair can do."

-- Sarah Manguso

"The self-confidence of the warrior is not the self-confidence of the average man. The average man seeks certainty in the eyes of the onlooker and calls that self-confidence. The warrior seeks impeccability in his own eyes and calls that humbleness. The average man is hooked to his fellow men, while the warrior is hooked only to infinity."

-- Carlos Castaneda

The number 8 of infinity appears throughout the sports world. More often than not it plays a central figure in the sport where it is found.

- Eight-ball pocket billiards is played with a cue ball and 15 numbered balls, the black ball numbered 8 being the middle and most important one. The winner is the player that legally pockets it after pocketing its numerical group of 7 object balls.

- The expression `behind the eight ball' means to be in a difficult or baffling situation.

- Balklines divide a billiards table into eight outside compartments or divisions called balks. In balkline billiards the table also has eight anchor spaces.

- In football, the number 8 has historically been the number of the Central Midfielder.

- In baseball scorekeeping, the center fielder is designated as number 8.

- In rugby union, the only position without a proper name is the Number 8, a forward position.

- In most rugby league competitions, one of the two starting props wears the number 8.

- In rowing an "eight" refers to a sweep-oar racing boat with a crew of eight rowers plus a coxswain. An eight is a racing boat with eight oars. Its crew is also called an eight. There are eight people in a tug-of-war team.

The power of infinity comes into play in the peak performance of athletes who rely on bodily movement in the same way that dancers flow from three dimensional form to four dimensional movement. The key to peak performance lies in the infinity zone where the groove of relaxed tension brings maximum effectiveness.

An example of this principle can be seen in the martial arts where there are many flowing figure 8 movements. One of the most powerful is the basic martial arts punch which starts in a horse stance. The feet are placed a bit wider than the shoulders with the knees bent, lowering the body for greater grounding and balance. With fists clenched at the hips, palms up, the punch begins from the

ground up, turning the hips, putting the whole body into it. While rotating the hips in the first movement of a figure 8, the fist comes forward, rotating as it extends in the beginning of a figure 8 of the arm that piggy backs on the energy of the turning hips, adding to its power.

At the end of the punch the hips are turned, with the arm extended at the end of its 180 degree twist. All of the energy is focused on the first two knuckles of the fist, effectively snapping the body and arm like a bullwhip, with the snap concentrated at the tip, completing the first half of the figure 8. The second half finishes on the return to the starting point. In practicing, both fists alternate in dual figure 8's.

The center of the human body's infinity zone where the hips turn revolves around what is called the dantian which occurs around the point on the body where the golden ratio makes it cut. Where the distance between the navel and the foot is taken as **1** unit, the height of a human being is equivalent to **1.618**.

Traditionally, the dantian is considered to be a center of qi or life

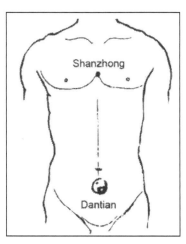

force energy and is an important point of reference in neidan, qigong, neigong, tao yin and other self-cultivation practices of exercise, breathing, and meditation, as well as in martial arts and traditional Chinese medicine. The lower dantian is particularly important as the focal point of breathing technique as well as the center of balance and gravity.

Taoist and Buddhist teachers often instruct their students to center the mind in the navel or lower dantian which is believed to aid control of thoughts and emotions. Acting from the dantian is considered to be related to higher states of awareness or samadhi.

The Taoist concept of dantians as energy centers is similar to the Indian yoga concept of chakras as key points through where prana is stored.

When a baseball pitcher throws the ball, the same dynamic is at work with his body and his pitching arm. The movement that comes into play from start to finish in a pitch is a figure 8 that delivers the ball with maximum speed and control.

Ice skaters move their body and legs in alternating figure **8**'s for optimum velocity and precise control. Speed skaters are the masters of this.

Olympic downhill skiers utilize side to side full body figure **8** movements to navigate steep declines with top precision, form, and speed. Those who master it are the ones who win competitions.

Fly fisherman cast their lines in a visible, repeating and expanding figure **8** motion that sends the fly sailing to its furthest reaches with the greatest accuracy.

Rowing boats, paddling canoes, and kayaks all use a figure **8** motion similar to the movement of a hummingbird's wings bringing the greatest power into each stroke of the oar or paddle.

The most complex utilization of the Infinity Zone comes into play in the game of tennis where the movement of the two players brings in multiple interrelated movements as well as a dynamic instantaneous flow of projective geometry on physical, mental, and emotional levels.

Rudolf Steiner uncovered geometric principles in his studies of projective geometry and spatial dynamics that laid the groundwork for the figure 8 that comes into play in the flight of the tennis ball and the movement of the racket, as tennis pros track the ball into their strings. Top players raise their hitting arm up as the ball rises over the net, rounding the corner and continuing up into the follow through, in a sideways figure **8**. Andre Agassi, Pete Sampras, Justine Henin, Marcelo Rios and Marat Safin all emulate this. In the greats like Agassi and Federer, a large figure **8** manifests in the hitting arm, initiated by a small figure **8** in the hips.

Additionally, a **45°** angle and its relationship to infinity is everywhere in tennis, beginning with the fact that it is the optimal contact point of every shot in the game. Moving the hips in a perfect figure 8 and keeping a coil in the arms results in a beautiful, seamless swing. Making contact with the ball this way also alleviates stress or strain in the body, because the hit is absorbed equally throughout the body. Top players understand and feel this synergy of a full-body swing, rippling out to the racket head at the point of contact.

This non-linear motion of the infinity zone can be seen throwing or hitting a baseball, throwing or kicking a football, hitting a tennis forehand, backhand or serve, serving or spiking a volleyball, or driving a golf ball.

This same motion can enhance any athlete's performance.

EIGHT

PRACTICAL APPLICATION OF THE INFINITY ZONE

"Our minds are finite, and yet even in these circumstances of finitude we are surrounded by possibilities that are infinite, and the purpose of life is to grasp as much as we can out of that infinitude"

-- Alfred North Whitehead

"It seemed to be a necessary ritual that he should prepare himself for sleep by meditating under the solemnity of the night sky... a mysterious transaction between the infinity of the soul and the infinity of the universe."

-- Victor Hugo

Gifted athletes perform the figure **8** motion intuitively in almost every sport or physical activity. They know it by feel, or as being "in the zone". People call them natural athletes because their entire bodies engage in the most efficient, fluid, and seamless flow of motion, resulting in effortless power, control, and grace. This unseen dynamic motion and balance is what makes great athletes stand out from the rest.

This infinity motion is considered the mother-form of all natural movement, particularly in natural athletes. Whether throwing or kicking a ball, swinging a bat, swinging a racquet, or a golf club, good athletes know that a tremendous amount of speed and power can be generated without ever having to move their arms or legs through  simple core-body rotation, which creates coordinated centrifugal force and inertia that initiates power and swing from the core.

Gifted athletes rotate their core differently from good athletes, causing a noticeably different motion throughout their entire body, causing them to move their arms and legs differently as well.

 Unlike the simple semi-circle hip or core rotation, exceptional athletes rotate their hips in a slow continuous figure **8**, causing their arms and legs to be pulled, creating a coil effect that expands, intensifying in energy from the body's core out to the apex of the throw, hit, or kick. This motion of the body, arms and/or legs is similar to a bullwhip, continuously and rapidly gaining speed. While the hand may only be traveling at **30-40** mph, the tip of the whip breaks the sound barrier at over **600** mph. Top athletes generate this speed and power through their understanding of dynamic balance and the geometric principles of non-linear motion.

According to tennis pro, Jack Broudy, the difference between the forehands of Andy Roddick and Roger Federer tell us much. Roddick's forehand stroke is good, but Federer's is a level up. Roddick's forehand stroke consists of a big, wide swing that is relatively the same speed throughout, whereas Federer's is smaller and slower in the beginning, with all the speed happening at contact. It has more power and efficiency.

Roger Federer's Forehand

No matter how fast Roddick swings at the ball he cannot produce the same racket head speed as Federer, who uses a slow whip-like motion initiated from his hips. Roddick simply swings fast, more by strength and will, primarily from his upper body, in a semi-circle.

The difference between their forehands is in the geometry of their strokes, and is tantamount to what separates the two players from good from great. Think of the figure **8** on both a horizontal and vertical plane with the figure-**8** motion as the source of energy that creates centrifugal force and a resulting sine wave that emanates out in concentric waves.

This figure **8** done in one continuous motion will elevate *any* person's level of performance in *any* sport. One of the keys to it is a slow, continuous movement starting in the hips and emanating out to the entire body. This furls and unravels the arms and/or legs in a non-linear fashion, producing immense speed and power with complete control and little effort.

This motion is equally represented in both the horizontal and vertical axis, left and right sides, and concentrically moves through the entire body like a human sine-wave, connecting everything into one motion.

People have become one-sided dominant, linear thinkers. The non-linear figure **8** can free them to perform beyond personal limitations, bringing a connection that synchronizes the entire body.

Tennis professionals Paul Mayberry and Jack Broudy combined their expertise and talent to develop a device called the 8Board that makes the magic of this revolutionary breakthrough in geometry and physics accessible to everyone.

Grail Sports 8Board

The **8**Board is a product of their company, Grail Sports Inc. that facilitates the integration of mind and body. Grail Sports has several design patents of the 8Board, as well as a utility patent on the learning of sports on two free-flowing swivels. It is the contention of Grail Sports that the proper learning of sports should begin at the core, then transfer out to the arms and legs.

Until now, sports have had the opposite approach, teaching the movement of the arms and then acquiring the natural flow of the body through hours and hours of practice. Anyone who has taken a tennis, golf, or baseball lesson understands this.

Since its conception in **1998**, the **8**Board has been used for everything from injury rehabilitation and sports training to weight loss and meditation. In the beginning, its primary use was to help athletes develop balance and coordination for golf and tennis.

Now the **8**Board system is a collection of data that contributes to an insightful and comprehensive science of flow, form, and function through the correlation between non-linear movement and the dynamics of space.

Relationships such as gravity levity the vertical and horizontal axis. The concept of infinity comes into play when describing the waving of a flag or the ripple of Agassi's backhand. The same laws of physics that apply to the progressions of a whip cracking, or a surfer ripping through a wave, can be seen in Federer's all-court game. Just as with nature itself, the effortless and powerful game of professional athletes is more than meets the eye.

Like the shaft of tree that barely blows in the wind, while the branches sway at the top and create all the movement, it is the little movement at the core that creates the big movement at the periphery. The **8**board allows people to feel this natural motion and begin their kinesthetic learning.

8Board Core Power Movement

As has been demonstrated, the power of the hit is not just in the arm, but a result of counter-balance of the lower body. Watching top players, it is obvious that the arm is always being dragged into the stroke by the hips.

Natural athleticism is about the proper path of the core. Radical improvements to this from using the **8**board became apparent within minutes of training. Mayberry and Broudy's students climbed their way up the tennis ladder, ranking number one in the United States in several of the junior age groups. Word spread of the benefits of the **8**board, and shortly thereafter the USC Tennis Team's coach, Peter Smith began to use the **8**Board in his and his players training. Now UNC Men's Tennis, Pepperdine, The San Diego Padres, UCLA Men's Golf Team, and other top professional and college players use the 8board in their training programs, both on and off court.

The figure **8** infinity movement can transform your thinking and your game, bringing dramatic improvements in your skills, your body, and your life. You will feel centered and balanced from using it, and your new-found quality of motion will translate into everything you do. You'll feel the sensation of dynamic balance and power running from your hips throughout your entire body equally and you will sense how your lower body affects your upper body. You will also feel your core and inner thighs become more centered, at the same time becoming more activated. Best of all, you'll learn to center and calm your mind, so you can perform your best without fear on a daily basis.

8boarding is a mind-body exercise that can benefit anyone in many ways, allowing your body to flow holistically, affecting everything from your wrists and elbows to your shoulders, legs, and low back. Your coordination and balance will improve everyday with little practice.

Fitness, in its highest form, includes a development of better balance, coordination, ambidexterity and athleticism. Instead of isolating muscles, it is better to integrate them and coordinate their movements. The mind body connection is what puts you *in the zone*.

When the body uses the hips as the core of the figure 8 motion, the left and the right sides of the body are balanced. The symmetry of movement enhances abilities, making them more coordinated. This figure 8 throughout the body is the essence of the natural throwing motion at the core of most sports, and the benefits of the 8Board are limitless.

In transforming your body, the 8Board burns calories, loosens joints, and stretches muscles without risk of injury caused by straining. Unlike any other product, it helps develop full-body balance, coordination, and ambidexterity.

In transforming your game, the 8board enhances skills in virtually any sport and other coordination-based activities. In addition to providing balance, it centers the body, enabling it to coil and respond quickly and naturally. It not only helps build muscle memory, it increases your awareness of what you're doing.

During this repetitive movement, you gain insight into what it means to be in *dynamic balance*, learning to stay centered while moving, staying conscious of your vertical axis staying over the center of the 8board. As many golfers know, sway is probably the biggest faux pas in amateur golf. When a player loses the integrity of balance, by falling off their vertical axis, they can no longer swing smoothly and evenly, and both power and control suffer. Worse than poor play, injuries are almost certain to increase because of improper mechanics.

The 8Board helps perfect one of the most essential skills of all athletes, the hip/body connection. Any athlete who swings a racquet, bat, or golf club knows that fluid power and control come from the balanced, twisting motion of the hips.

The revolutionary concept of the **8**Board is dynamic balance which comes through movement. Several lessons on it will teach you to feel your body's center as your hips create a figure **8** motion orbiting around that center. You will feel how dynamic balance is a state of natural, total body coordination.

As you do the Figure **8** motion, you will feel your hips pull your arms and feet into motion, as opposed to your hands initiating the movement. As one hip rises, the other will fall in a constant flow of motion taking place due to the weight transfer, verticality, and horizontal movement, while maintaining your center.

The **8**Board is used by professional athletes in baseball, golf, volleyball, tennis, snowboarding, skiing, and football. Some of the nation's leading coaches use it to train athletes. PGA Director of Instruction, John Mason, **2005** SCPGA Teacher of the Year, and **2002** SDPGA Player of the Year uses the **8**Board to train his students at the JC Golf School in Encinitas, California. Since implementing the figure **8** techniques, many of his students have shown signs of greater club control, strength, power, accuracy, and range.

Mason says, "The **8**Board will give you the feeling of what proper balance and rotational flexibility feels like, in a matter of minutes. I use it everyday and recommend it to all my students."

In addition to helping with balance, the **8**Board promotes graceful movement and helps connect the body to the earth. Many seniors use it to improve and maintain their balance and posture. Most linear exercises like running on a treadmill or lifting free weights require minimal coordination or even interest.

Unique in its genre, the **8**Board is structured around non-linear motion. By doing the figure **8** on an **8**board you can feel any imbalances in your body, its availability of movement, and make the necessary corrections to balance things out. When your motion feels effortless and balanced, you know you're doing it right.

The **8**Board circulates your entire body, and promotes flexibility and balance, which will help you get in touch with your athletic side. When doing the infinity movement correctly, every part of the body is engaged, from the knees and arms to the hips and back with all muscles and joints flowing together like liquid.

Aside from radically improved athletic performance, the 8board has been instrumental in healing debilitating sports injuries.

Liz Masakayan

Women's Olympic Volleyball Team medalist, Liz Masakayan used the **8**board to rehabilitate a knee injury. After six reconstructive knee surgeries, Liz says that the **8**Board was the most effective tool she used to restore her ankles and knees. In Liz's words, "In order to take the pressure off my knees, I get on the **8**Board to loosen up my hips and to get my whole core more flexible.

It is an excellent movement for injury rehab and pain prevention. Working out on the 8Board has helped me to enhance the proper functional movements that I need to perform all of my skills more effectively from my core with more grace and power."

During his **35**-year professional career, Golf instructor Russ Fraser has taught at Ojai Valley Inn and Country Club, Florida's Alhambra Golf Club and at The Lakes of El Segundo, California. Russ has competed in eight PGA Qualifying Tours and was a finalist at the **1975** U.S. Open. What follows is his personal story on how the Figure **8** and **8**board dramatically changed his life.

"As a golf professional and professional golfer my legs and physical health have become more important as I age gracefully.

In **1977**, while playing a practice round before a tournament, I severely tore my medial meniscus ligament of my left leg. Long story short, after not having surgery and playing on an injured leg, my leg health deteriorated to a point where I had to have surgery in **1984**. The surgery removed most of the medial meniscus ligament that was remaining and the surgeon had filed the femur to fit the area that was affected. I did little or no rehab after surgery and went back to teaching golf as I thought my playing days were over.

Russ Fraser

In **2000**, I reached a point where a knee replacement was not too far down the road. I began to work out and practice the rehab I was supposed to do earlier. My leg became stronger but was not functioning effectively. Basically, it felt as if my left leg was dead or only functioned partially. I felt better with exercise and strength conditioning but it still was not right.

Then in early **2003** I met with Jack Broudy of Grail Sports. I had opened an indoor training center including a fitness gym. I was always looking for equipment that would help promote fitness and proper golf movement. The **8**Board seemed to be a great fit. With use of the instructional video, I took the **8**Board and began adding other items to enhance the work out. I used golf clubs, pole mops, weighted bars, and medicine balls. Then I added a resistance band which I attached to a fixed object. With the extra resistance of the bands, I worked my left side, leg and gluts.

After about **4** or **5** minutes of vigorous activity, a sensation like an electrical shock wave traveled up and down up my left leg. It didn't hurt, and in some ways, it was extremely exhilarating.

When I stepped off of the **8**Board, my left leg felt alive and energized for the first time in twenty years. It was as if new life had been poured into my legs. As I began walking around, it felt as if my left leg had been energized. I couldn't wait to tell someone.

I walked across the street to share the story with my friend, who also happens to be an exercise specialist by the name of Jay Sabol. At the time, he was a Level **3** Paul Chek therapist. I tried to explain what had happened and the sensation that was occurring and still going on. We could not come up with an explanation for the sensation or the dramatic change that had occurred in my leg. The leg felt stronger, to the point that walking was a pleasure again.

The greatest benefit was what it did for my golf game. It brought back the sixty-yard drive that I had lost due to the inability to use and stabilize my left leg while swinging. For six years, I have been using the **8**Board. It has been a great addition to my teaching tools and has brought joy to my students. Other teachers at my facility use it and have seen the benefits in creating better understanding of dynamic movement during the golf swing.

Every session is started with an **8**Board warm up, and I use it to create the mental sensation of dynamic balance and proper synchronicity. It also helps my students understand the term 'grounded' and how ground-force dynamics applies to the sport. Most importantly, the **8**Board works on the body and calms the spirit. Nothing else has been as effective for my rehabilitation as the

8Board."

Linda Goulart from Carlsbad California wrote the following.
"Hi my name is Linda,

In **2011** my left leg was amputated above the knee. The goal of balance, strength and movement have been my on going challenges. I fell constantly, losing my balance when I would try to twist to do things as simple as closing a door or looking over my shoulder when someone called my name. My therapist helped me with improving my basic balance but I still had the problem of falling when a fluid movement was required.

The therapist introduced me to the 8board. After just two times of using it I noticed a HUGE IMPROVEMENT! After two more times the falling problem was solved. I now have my own **8**board at home and use it twice a day, each time for just a few minutes. The **8**board has brought back continuous, fluid movement and the ability to finesse my balance and stiffening up.

I have been able to work in my garden again and I no longer loose my balance. I can close a the car door and not fall. I can work in the kitchen and not fall. All these things are easily taken for granted - I was not able to do any successfully without the 8board.
Thank you from the bottom of my heart.
Linda"

Due to its ability to improve balance, flexibility, coordination and ambidexterity, the **8**Board is used by martial arts studios, chiropractors, occupational therapists, physical therapists, and weight loss clinics. Many trainers use it with a variety of other exercise equipment including medicine balls, straps, bars and weights with amazing results. Many trainers feel there are major benefits in doing push ups with the hands on the swivels. The **8**Board is the perfect warm up for all sports and activities and it aids in preventing injury.

Recognized for its abundant benefits, the 8Board was voted among the Top Ten Training Aids by the PGTAA (Professional Golf Teachers Association of America), and has been featured on the NBC Evening News.

The possibilities that the 8board open up are infinite.

It increases:

- Balance
- Kinesthetic awareness
- Coordination
- Consistency
- Fluidity
- Body Rotation
- Awareness of Periphery
- Focus
- Control
- Strength and Power
- Accuracy and Range
- Gracefulness
- Connects the body and earth
- Centeredness
- Non-linear Movement
- Self-discovery
- Athletic Skills
- Circulation
- Stability of the joints in the lower body and torso
- Flexibility/mobility (passive and active)
- Core strength
- Body Engagement
- Functional power via grounding energy flow/transfer
- Muscle Memory
- Movement speed
- Quiets the body
  (allows non-moving parts to be at rest without tension or stress)
- Movement aptitude
- Low-impact exercise
- Rehabilitation
- Injury Prevention

It decreases:

- Hyper-mobility in lower torso and limbs
- Incidence of injury
- Severity of injury
- Recovery time (active and inactive)
- Rehab time and energy on the torso and lower limbs
- Back pain
- Spinal pain
- Headaches occurrence
- Headache severity
- Lost playing time
- Inconsistent play
- Short swings
- Tight hips/back/shoulders
- Limitations and excuses

The **8**Board's cultivation of the infinity zone can change the way you view your self and has been employed by brain injury victims and dyslexics to help develop motor skills, encompassing full-body coordination, ambidexterity, dynamic balance and flexibility and it has helped numerous athletes improve their consistency and learn to view the playing field in an entirely new dimension. It has also helped others re-establish their relationship with their bodies and minds.

Once practiced and understood, the Infinity Zone is realized as a higher state of consciousness that can be applied to achieve transcendent peak performance.

Its power is universal.

NINE

THE INFINITY ZONE
AS A HIGHER STATE OF CONSCIOUSNESS

"If the doors of perception were cleansed every thing would appear to man as it is, Infinite. For man has closed himself up, till he sees all things thro' narrow chinks of his cavern."

— William Blake

"Meditation is the dissolution of thoughts in Eternal awareness or Pure consciousness without objectification, knowing without thinking, merging finitude in infinity."

— Voltaire

After number eight, the number nine is the final single digit in our decimal system that precedes the next highest order, which is ten, symbolized by a one and a zero. It is the last digit preceding each progression of ten beyond that.

Additionally, our physical bodies are bilateral. We have ten toes and ten fingers with an opposable thumb; a distinct physical advantage that ranks us at the top of the earth's animal hierarchy with the higher primates. Physiologically our digits are a prime external indicator of our place at the top of the evolutionary scale, while internally, among other things, the  development of our brain charts the path of the evolution of our consciousness along its progression into self-awareness; the capability that distinguishes us above all other life forms on the earth.

The term consciousness refers to common capabilities of humans and other animals, as well as to differentiate between them, designating uniquely human linguistic, rational, and abstract capabilities. Consciousness also includes a range of functions that esoteric traditions claim supersede rational and egoic forms of consciousness, representing the evolution of what is conceptualized as spirit, soul, mind, self, and transcendental human capabilities.

Although human consciousness is not specific to any particular function or system of the brain, different modalities of consciousness are associated with different systemic information-processing functions, integration of brain processes, and patterns of homeostasis. All of the major systems of the brain participate in complex human behavior, but specific systemic patterns of brain functioning are associated with distinct experiential states and modes of consciousness. Recognition that consciousness is tied to the functioning of a biological system does not require reduction of consciousness solely to the functions of biological system.

A neurophenomenological approach illustrates that both epistemic constructs and physiological patterns of brain operation contribute to consciousness. The relationship of brain physiology to consciousness is illustrated through an examination of how the physical structures of the brain and their associated activities relate to patterns of consciousness.

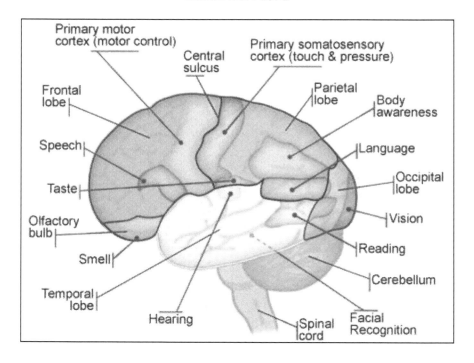

Brain Diagram of Cerebrum Functions

The brain can be viewed as three anatomically distinct systems that are integrated to provide a range of behavioral, emotional, and informational functions.

It is widely recognized that human motor patterns, emotional states, and advanced cognitive and linguistic capabilities are primarily managed by brain systems that emerged sequentially in evolution. This triune brain model provides a framework for explicating the relationship between systemic brain activities and consciousness, relating to lower brain systems common with other animals and to unique aspects of the human brain.

The hierarchical tripartite triune brain is based on neuroanatomical, structural, and functional divisions that break down into three strata starting with the reptilian, followed by the paleomammalian, and neomammalian brains. The three formations have different anatomical structures that mediate different psychological and behavioral functions, with their own forms of subjectivity, intelligence, time and space sense, memory capabilities, and motor functions. Although the three segments are integrated, they provide the bases for different capacities and represent a functional hierarchy of information-processing capabilities that provide the basis for distinct forms of consciousness.

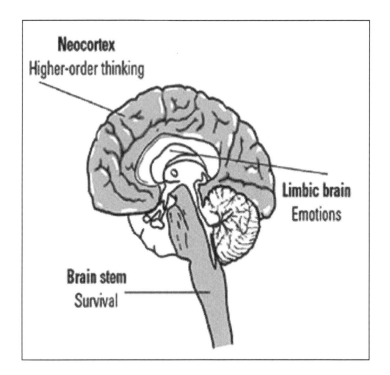

The Triune Brain

The reptilian brain is composed of the upper spinal cord, portions of mesencephalon (midbrain), diencephalon (thalamus-hypothalamus), and basal ganglia. The reptilian brain regulates organic functions such as metabolism, digestion, and respiration. It is also responsible for wakefulness, attentional mechanisms, and the regulation and coordination of behavior.

The paleomammalian brain is based on evolutionary developments in the limbic system, which provided for distinctions between reptiles and mammals. This structure provides the basis for social behavior and nonverbal, emotional, and analogical information processing, and it functions as an emotional brain, mediating affect; sex; fighting/self defense; social relations, bonding and attachment; and the sense of self that provides the basis for beliefs, certainty, and convictions.

The neomammalian brain provides the basis for advanced symbolic processes, culture, language, logic, rational thought, analytical processes, and complex problem solving.

The reptilian brain provides the basic plots and actions of the body. The paleomammalian brain provides the emotional influences on thoughts and behavior. The neomammalian brain uses enhanced symbolic capacities in elaborating on the basic plots and emotions and integrating them with higher-level information processing.

The reptilian brain provides the organism with primary or simple awareness, which is adaptation to the environment through reflexes, conditioned responses, and habituation, as well as through instrumental learning. The paleomammalian brain provides for qualities of consciousness enriched by self, other (society), and emotions, while the neomammalian brain encompassing the tertiary neocortical area and, in particular, the right hemisphere, are involved in cross-integration and reorganization of perceptual modalities and are basic to symbolic cognition and self-awareness. The neomammalian brain (neocortex and connecting thalamic structures) represents the most dramatic evolution of the brain. The expanded neocortex's functions are based on extensive connections with the visual, auditory, and somatic systems, indicating the primary orientation of the neocortex to the external world.

These three structures are also referred to as the three centers that we principally operate from, known from the top down as intellectual, emotional, and moving, that form a triad that relates to the every day functioning of our personality. These centers act as primary energizers and determine the way that a person generally responds to any stimuli.

A moving centered person will tend to be physically active and be fond of sports, travel, and action.

An emotionally centered person will tend to be more perceptive and will experience situations in terms of likes and dislikes.

An intellectually centered person will tend to be more verbal and will enjoy philosophy and thinking for its own sake.

Most people react from one of these centers. When presented with any situation, their first immediate response will be either thought, feeling, or action, which represents the center they habitually rely on. If they react with thought they are intellectually centered, if they respond with feeling, they are emotionally centered, and if they respond with instantaneous action, they are moving centered.

People usually respond out of these three centers in a specific order. If they are intellectually centered they will first react with thought, emotions will follow, then they will act. If they are emotionally centered they will feel first, act, then think about it later. Any combination of the three is possible as a habitual pattern based on their most developed center which comes first, and their least developed which comes last. The closer a person comes to operating simultaneously out of all three centers, the more integrated and effective they are.

When a person is paying attention, being fully aware, such as they are when they are in the Infinity Zone, they are more likely to feel, think, and act simultaneously. From this balanced point of power, fears are neutralized and experience shifts to insight, relatedness, and beauty. Intentional awakening is fostered by the perception that one has not achieved one's potential. In order to reach higher levels of awareness (Maslow's peak experience), three conditions are necessary; a powerful desire to know the truth, a willingness to be emotionally open to life, and a practiced ability to be balanced energetically. Intellectual, emotional, and moving centers form a triad which relates to the universal building blocks of love, energy, and truth, otherwise known as, love, power, and wisdom; a triad that manifests as inspiration, action, and expression.

A natural result of the evolution of the human brain is the fragmentation of consciousness, reflecting both the increasing modularity of consciousness and the diversification of self into more statuses. Shamanic traditions institutionalized procedures to overcome this fragmentation of consciousness by synchronizing this divergent human cognition through traditions using altered states of consciousness (ASC) to induce integrative brain processes. The use of external symbols and the relationships of the symbols to cultural psychodynamics engage transformative process through entraining neurocognitive structures, provoking a restructuring of the self at levels below conceptual and operational thought.

Shamanistic practices induce extraordinary experiences and healing by producing integrative relationships among brain systems and psychocultural beliefs. These experiences reflect the simultaneous elicitation and integration of normal modes of information processing and consciousness that do not ordinarily occur together. These altered states nonetheless involve normal integrative psychobiological processes elicited by many procedures.

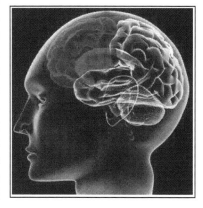

A primary focus of the psychophysiological effects of shamanistic ASC is in the limbic system, or the paleomammalian brain. This brain area emerged in the evolution of mammals and provided a number of distinctive developments. Shamanistic healing is based on manipulation of processes and functions of the paleomammalian brain – self identity and social identity and their attachments, emotions, meanings, and references. Shamanistic ASC elicit processes of the paleomammalian brain and induce a systemic integration of information processing functions across the functional layers of the brain, producing limbic-cortical integration and interhemispheric synchronization, best symbolized by a dynamic figure 8 infinity pattern.

Shamanistic healing practices achieve this integration by physically stimulating systematic brain wave discharge patterns that activate affects, memories, attachments, and other psychodynamic processes of the paleomammalian brain. This activation forces normally unconscious or preconscious primary information processing functions and outputs to be integrated into the operations of the frontal cortex. This integrates implicit understandings, socioemotional dynamics, repressed memories, unresolved conflicts, intuitions, and nonverbal – visual, mimetic, and presentational knowledge into self-conscious awareness.

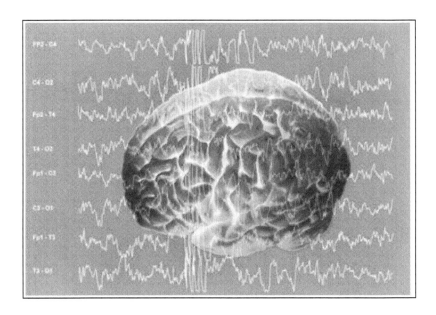

Activated Brain Wave Patterns

The desire to alter consciousness is an innate, human, biologically based drive with adaptive significance. The ASC of shamanism are a manifestation of a fundamental homeostatic dynamic of the nervous system. These manifestations of consciousness involve a biologically based integrative mode of consciousness, replacing normal waking conditions – sympathetic dominance and desynchronized fast wave activity of the frontal cortex – with a parasympathetic dominant state characterized by high voltage, slow-wave electroencephalogram (EEG) activity originating in the circuits linking the brain stem and the hippocampal-septal area of the limbic system with the frontal cortex. This high-voltage, slow wave EEG activity originates in the hippocampal-septal area and imposes a synchronous slow-wave pattern on the frontal lobes, producing interhemispheric synchronization and coherence, limbic-cortex integration, and integration across the neuraxis, a synthesis of behavior, emotion, and thought.

The parasympathetic state, slow-wave synchronization of the frontal cortex, and interhemispeheric integration reflect activation of basic aspects of brain operation related to sensory and physiological integration; mental and emotional integration; insight and transcendence; and interhemispheric integration.

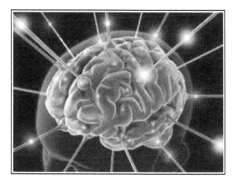

A primary characteristic of integrative consciousness within the Infinity Zone involves the hierarchical integration of brain mechanisms, especially as manifested in limbic system driving of the frontal cortex through serotonergic induced integration across the neuraxis.

This represents the integration of preconscious or unconscious functions and material into self conscious awareness.

There are four different biologically based modes of human consciousness – waking, sleep, dream, and integrative consciousness. These reflect the fundamental aspects of systemic functioning of the human organism that meet the following system functions and needs, respectively: learning, adaptation, and survival needs (waking); recuperative functions, regeneration, and growth (deep sleep); memory integration and consolidation and psychosocial adaptation (dreaming); and psychodynamic growth and social and psychological integration (integrative).

The right hemisphere of the brain reflects a different symbolic form of representation in dreaming than that used in waking consciousness. The bizarreness of dreams reflects the imaginative and creative capacities of the presentational modality. Dreams appear bizarre and illogical from the point of view of waking consciousness because dreams involve a different system of information representation, processing, and consolidation. This visual-spatial system of symbolic presentation is normally inhibited by the dominance of left-hemisphere verbal representational systems; conditions that attenuate the left hemisphere's verbal representational systems allow expression of this presentational intelligence.

Meditation, rituals, hallucinogens and other shamanic practices can alter consciousness and physiological processes through a wide variety of mechanisms that induce retuning of the autonomic nervous system balance. Working with an 8Board can produce similar results. This retuning tends to block the dominant hemisphere's functions and produces an integrative fusion with functions of the nondominant hemisphere; this structurally synchronized state tends to resolve internal conflicts and produce euphoric states. This synchronization depends on the elicitation of processes of lower brain structures that are associated with basic behavior, intentionality, and emotions, which is something that occurs in a tennis match.

These ASC evoke communicative responses from the paleomammalian brain that provide the basis for an expansion of consciousness by integrating information from the lower brain systems into operational activities of the frontal brain and by establishing synchrony with the frontal brain that permits symbolic reprogramming of the emotional dynamics and behavioral repertoires of lower brain centers.

When the triune brain works in unison and the individual operates simultaneously out of all three centers, the more integrated and effective they are because they will be fully aware. The instinctual, emotional, and intellectual centers will feel, think, and act simultaneously from a balanced point of power where fears are neutralized and experience shifts to insight, relatedness, and beauty.

When there is a homeostatic dynamic of the nervous system, a biologically based integrative mode of consciousness comes into play, replacing normal waking conditions – sympathetic dominance and desynchronized fast wave activity of the frontal cortex with a parasympathetic dominant state, producing interhemispheric synchronization and coherence, and integration across the neuraxis, synthesizing behavior, emotion, and thought. The parasympathetic state, slow-wave synchronization of the frontal cortex, and interhemispeheric integration reflect activation of basic aspects of brain operation related to sensory and physiological integration; mental and emotional integration; and insight and transcendence. In essence, the slow-wave synchronization of the frontal cortex is the energy that comes from transcending the male and female polarities, creating a triad that focuses on the energy manifest in between as opposed to that of the extremes.

Three brains from the top down working in unison to produce a fully aware state of insight, relatedness, and beauty, combined with the right "female" brain and the left "male" brain working in synchronization and coherence, synthesizing behavior, emotion, and thought to produce a slow-wave synchronization of the third frontal cortex indicate sensory and physiological integration; mental and emotional integration; and insight and transcendence.

Integration, Insight, and Transcendence

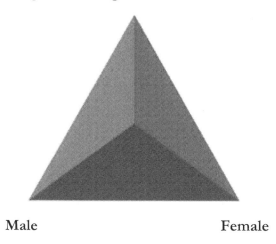

Male   Female

Fully Integrated 3 x 3 Brain

This fully turned on **3 x 3** brain brings a radical shift in consciousness that could produce a shift from our present fourth dimensional existence that perceives a three dimensional world, to the fifth dimension where we perceive the fourth dimension, transcending time and duality.

If we are aware enough to be in harmony with the natural unfolding cosmic laws of oneness, reciprocity, and balance, and we are in harmony and alignment within ourselves, living in full integrity and unity with all that is, we will ride the wave, flow forward, and become fully conscious co-creators of our reality, operating from our place of power, the Infinity Zone.

TEN

TO INFINITY AND BEYOND

"Does there exist an Infinity outside ourselves? Is that infinity One, immanent and permanent, necessarily having substance, since He is infinite and if He lacked matter He would be limited, necessarily possessing intelligence since He is infinite and, lacking intelligence, He would be in that sense finite. Does this Infinity inspire in us the idea of essense, while to ourselves we can only attribute the idea of existence? In order words, is He not the whole of which we are but the part?"

– Victor Hugo

"To infinity and beyond."

-- Buzz Lightyear

Infinity is part of the great cosmic mystery that pushes the limits of everything we know, which by its very nature is finite. As soon as we try to define infinity, it loses its meaning by the very attempt at definition, which tries to contain that which cannot be bounded. It is a paradox, which as we have seen in the Infinity Zone, is where our consciousness is centered in a place in the cosmos that contains power, mystery, and universal wisdom that becomes apparent through the perception of higher consciousness.

Unseen yet perceived, it defines the ancient wisdom of, "as above, so below", and though unseen and pointing toward the unknown, it resides within us; the living, breathing, dynamic manifestation of the nexus between the third and fourth dimensions of time and space.

The center of the Universe is right between our eyes.

Though physically intangible, the magic of its power is available to us by understanding and cultivating its combined properties of dynamic form and motion through the vehicle of our consciousness, our body; the vessel that carries us on our journey through the third dimension.

It is the place where spirit meets matter.

Its mystery has been contemplated and recognized throughout history.

In Buddhism, the **8**-spoked Dharmacakra represents the Noble Eightfold Path.

The Dharmacakra, a Buddhist Symbol, has Eight Spokes

Division	Eightfold Path factors	Acquired factors
Wisdom (Sanskrit: *prajñā*, Pāli: *paññā*)	1. Right view	9. Superior right knowledge
	2. Right intention	10. Superior right liberation
Ethical conduct (Sanskrit: *śīla*, Pāli: *sīla*)	3. Right speech	
	4. Right action	
	5. Right livelihood	
Concentration (Sanskrit and Pāli: *samādhi*)	6. Right effort	
	7. Right mindfulness	
	8. Right concentration	

The Buddha'sNoble Eightfold Path

In Mahayana Buddhism, the branches of the Eightfold Path are embodied by the Eight Great Bodhisattvas:

- Manjusri
- Vajrapani
- Avalokitesvara
- Maitreya
- Ksitigarbha
- Nivaranavishkambhi
- Akasagarbha
- Samantabhadra

These are later associated with the Eight Consciousnesses according to the Yogacara school of thought: consciousness in the five senses, thought-consciousness, self-consciousness, and unconsciousness-'consciousness' (alaya-vijñana). The irreversible state of enlightenment, at which point a Bodhisattva goes on autopilot, is the Eight Ground or *bhūmi*. In general, eight seems to be an auspicious number for Buddhists, e.g., the eight auspicious symbols, the jewel-encrusted parasol; the goldfish, always shown as a pair, e.g., the glyph of Pisces; the self-replenishing amphora; the white *kamala* lotus-flower; the white conch; the eternal, Celtic-style, infinitely looping knot; the banner of imperial victory; the eight-spoked wheel that guides the ship of state, or symbolizes the Buddha's teaching. Similarly, Buddha's birthday falls on the **8**th day of the **4**th month of the Chinese calendar.

In superstition and divination the number **8** sign of infinity appears as a lucky number.

Eight (八; accounting 捌; pinyin *bā*) is considered a lucky number in Chinese culture because it sounds like the word meaning to generate wealth (發(T) 发(S); Pinyin: *fā*).

Property with the number **8** may be valued greatly by Chinese. A Hong Kong number plate with the number **8** was sold for **$640,000**.

In the **2008** Games of the XXIX Olympiad, the official opening was on **08/08/08** at **8:08:08** p.m. local time in Beijing, China.

Eight (八 *hachi, yá?*) is also considered a lucky number in Japanese culture, but the reason is different from Chinese culture. Eight gives an idea of growing prosperous, because the letter (八) broadens gradually.

The Japanese thought eight (や *yá?*) as a holy number in the ancient times. The reason is less well understood, but it is thought that it is related to the fact they used eight to express large numbers vaguely such as manyfold, やえはたえ *Yae Hatae?* literally eightfold and twentyfold, many clouds やくも *Yakumo?* literally eight clouds, millions and millions of Gods やおよろずのかみ *Yaoyorozu no Kami?* literally, eight millions of Gods, etc.

It is also guessed that the ancient Japanese gave importance to pairs, so some researchers guess twice as four, よ *yo?*, which is also guessed to be a holy number in those times because it indicates that the world, north, south, east, and west might be considered a very holy number.

In numerology, **8** is the number of building, and in some theories, also the number of destruction. In astrology, in the Middle Ages, 8 was the number of "unmoving" stars in the sky, and symbolized the perfectioning of incoming planetary energy.

In the world as we know it, space is the final frontier and the mind's capacity to observe and experience a more holistic conception of it is the quest. In the works of Rudolf Steiner he describes a state of consciousness where a different kind of space is experienced. One that is polar opposite to our ordinary euclidian conception. Such a consciousness looks in from the periphery towards an unreachable inwardness, in contrast to the normal experience which looks out from a center towards an unreachable outwardness. This point of view allows the possibility to perceive a rarefied environment called counter-space.

Through the precise mathematical processes of projective geometry it is possible to experience the world we call the Infinity Zone.

This polar-euclidian space has a different metric basis and is free of the usual limitations of ordinary space. With the realization that counter-space is a component of reality one can harness this extra spatial perception in every activity one engages in and transcend the one-sided linear mentality that predominates to experience the connected qualitative holistic dynamic realm of the Infinity Zone.

It is in this realm of unlimited perception that the tools of super-coordination exist. This counter-space continuum reveals how all space is connected in a web and that through a symbol of a path we call the figure **8**, we can connect to all of space and time through a dynamic motion that balances the whole body synchronously. When we link our objective movements with the subjective experience of our own processes we confirm when we are in-sync, and when we are lost in space.

In competition we feel confident when we are in control of the situation and can project the outcome, yet the process is more important than the outcome. When we focus on the intangible elements of infinity, it is possible to become self creative, and all empowering. This new found awareness liberates us from the cause and effect world that breaks us down and alienates us from our true roots in the cosmos.

Works Cited

Broudy, Jack W. The Real Spin on Tennis: Grasping the Mind, Body, and Soul of the Game. Washington, D.C.: ICS Publications, 1997.

Friedman, Robert L. The Healing Power of the Drum. Incline Village, White Cliffs Media Company, 2000.

MacLean, P. The Triune Concept of Brain and Behavior.
    Toronto: University of Toronto Press, 1973.
_____. The Triune Brain in Evolution.
New York: Plenum Press, 1990.

Nicoll, Maurice. Psychological Commentaries on the Teachings of Gurdjieff & Ouspensky. London: Watkins, 1980.

Olsen, Scott. The Golden Section: Nature's Greatest Secret. New York: Walker and Company, 2006.
_____. Divine Proportion: The Mathematical Perfection of the Universe, New York: Walker and Company, 2013.

Schwaller de Lubicz, R. A.. The Temple in Man, Rochester: Inner Traditions, 1981.
_____. The Temple of Man, Rochester: Inner Traditions, 1998.

Steiner, Rudolph. The Fourth Dimension: Sacred Geometry, Alchemy, and Mathematics. Great Barrington: Anthroposophic Press, 2001.

Stevens, José. Earth to Tao.
Santa Fe: Bear and Company, 1994.

Thomas, Nick. Science Between Space And Counterspace. London: New Science Books, 1999.

Winkelman, Michael. Shamanism: The Neural Ecology of Consciousness and Healing. Westport: Bergin & Garvey, 2000.

URLS

www.grailsports.com
www.schooloftennis.net
www.mattpallamary.com
www.mysticinkpublishing.com

Counter Space
http://www.nct.anth.org.uk/counter.htm

Dance
http://en.wikipedia.org/wiki/Contra_dance_choreography

Fish
http://www.people.fas.harvard.edu/~glauder/reprints_unzipped/FishLauder2006.pdf

Harmony
http://en.wikipedia.org/wiki/Harmony

Hummingbirds
http://www.ehow.com/how-does_4566089_a-hummingbird-fly.html#ixzz1nRkn8szJ
http://www.birdfeeders.com/resources/wild-bird-articles/hummingbirds/to-catch-a-hummingbird
http://www.nectarartprints.com/hb_flight.htm
http://www.hummingbirds.net/images/figure8.mov
http://clackhi.nclack.k12.or.us/physics/projects/rates_around_us/hummingbird%20Folder/hummingbirds.htm
http://hummingbirdworld.com/h/behavior.htm
http://www.youtube.com/watch?v=x3th_3BZVHQ
http://www.youtube.com/watch?v=ils4cqeekSI
http://www.bbc.co.uk/nature/life/Hummingbird#p00cn9h7
http://www.instructables.com/id/Figure-Eight-Motion-Drive/
http://jeb.biologists.org/content/210/13/2368.full.pdf
http://blogs.bu.edu/biolocomotion/2011/10/21/its-a-bird-no-its-an-insect-no-wait-its-a-hummingbird/

Infinity

http://en.wikipedia.org/wiki/Infinity
http://www.goodreads.com/quotes/tag/infinity
http://f06.middlebury.edu/FYSE1176A/Infinity_Quotes.html

Insects

http://www.everythingabout.net/articles/biology/animals/arthropo
ds/insects/
http://www.insectman.us/articles/misc-design/flight/testimony-
creation.htm
http://www.bumblebee.org/bodyEyehtm.htm
http://insects.about.com/od/antsbeeswasps/p/honeybeecommun.h
tm
http://www.ehow.com/facts_5180742_butterfly-wings.html

Music

http://en.wikipedia.org/wiki/Musica_universalis

Number 8

http://www.virtuescience.com/8.html
http://en.wikipedia.org/wiki/8_(number)
http://richardphillips.org.uk/number/Num8.htm
http://www.ridingthebeast.com/numbers/nu8.php
http://mysticalnumbers.com/Number_8.html
http://numerology-
thenumbersandtheirmeanings.blogspot.com/2011/05/number-
8.html
http://en.wikipedia.org/wiki/Apollo_8

Sacred Geometry

http://en.wikipedia.org/wiki/Sacred_geometry
http://www.goldennumber.net/
http://milan.milanovic.org/math/english/body/
http://www.software3d.com/Stella.php

Paul Mayberry was a top junior Tennis player who now coaches players all over the world. His interests include invention, music, coaching, and philosophy, with an emphasis on the mathematics and philosophy of Rudolf Steiner. His interests and passion led to his co-founding Grail Sports Inc.

Paul has developed a number of inventions, his most renowned being the Grail Sports 8board. Aside from coaching, Paul spends his time promoting and teaching the use of the 8board and its practical applications. He is a Gemini, the 3rd sign of the zodiac and the 9 of clubs in the Birthcard Astrology system.

GRAILSPORTS.COM

Matthew Pallamary's historical novel **Land Without Evil,** received rave reviews along with a San Diego Book Award for mainstream fiction. Matt also received the Man of the Year 2000 award from San Diego Writer's Monthly Magazine. **Dreamland,** a novel about computer generated dreaming, written with Ken Reeth, won the 2002 Independent e-Book Award in the Horror/Thriller category.

His memoir **Spirit Matters** detailing his journeys to Peru, working with shamanic plant medicines took first place in the San Diego Book Awards Spiritual Book Category, and was an Award-Winning Finalist in the autobiography/memoir category of the National Best Books 2008 Awards. He is a Scorpio, the 8th sign of the zodiac and the 8 of clubs in the Birthcard Astrology system.

WWW.MATTPALLAMARY.COM

BOOKS BY MATTHEW J. PALLAMARY

THE SMALL DARK ROOM OF THE SOUL

LAND WITHOUT EVIL

SPIRIT MATTERS

DREAMLAND (WITH KEN REETH)

A SHORT WALK TO THE OTHER SIDE

APPENDIX

The **8**Board is the ultimate tennis training device, but beyond tennis it is the ultimate body-motion trainer that helps perfect one of the most essential skills of all athletes – the hip/body connection. Any competitive athlete who swings a racquet, a bat, or a golf club knows that fluid power and control come from the balanced, twisting motion of the hips. What top athletes all have in common is balance throughout their swings. This fluid, powerful, controlled movement can be perfected by anyone.

The **8**Board uses a series of exercises that are *non-linear* in nature. Most linear exercises, such as running on a treadmill or lifting free weights, require minimal coordination. Unique in its genre, the **8**Board is structured around non-linear motion. Doing the figure **8** on an **8**board allows you to feel any imbalances in your body, and its availability of movement, so you can make the corrections necessary to balance things out.

To improve balance and coordination with the **8**board, as opposed to other forms of exercise, it is actually "slowness" that helps you to feel and correct your body's motion. The more slowly you move, the more creative you become. Slow motion gives your body a chance to experience the inner quality of the movement. Subtle movement versus the flash of speed gives you a more definable quality in your motion. Slow movement opens up a world of inner thought and effortlessness. When your motion feels effortless and balanced, you know you're doing it right.

When doing the figure **8** movement correctly, *every part of the body is engaged*. From the knees and arms to the hips and back, all muscles and joints are flowing together like liquid.

The **8**board is adjustable. For most people averaging **5'3"** to **6'1"**, adjustment **#3** works best, which is approximately shoulder width apart. If you feel more comfortable at a different adjustment, do what feels best, but if the **8**board is too wide or too narrow it will be difficult for your hips to move in a figure **8**.

Eight Simple Steps To Using The 8Board

1. Stand directly behind the board. Slowly place your feet on the two swivels with your toes facing forward. Feel free to hold onto a chair or any stationary object if you need support.

2. Bend your knees slightly so that your legs are not locked at the joints. Your feet should be approximately shoulder width apart.

3. Face forward and try not to look down at your feet. It is critical that your vertical access stays true, in line. Don't lean in any direction and keep your back straight.

4. Interlace your fingers, pressing together your thumbs and index fingers. Your index fingers will work as an imaginary pencil, drawing geometric forms in the air. Keep your elbows bent -- pressed firmly against your rib cage with your arms perpendicular to your torso.

5. Slowly begin drawing a horizontal line in front of you, right to left and then left to right, keeping your elbows pressed against your rib cage. Keeping your elbows pinned to your ribcage will force your legs to follow the movement of your arms.

6. Your feet will begin to move parallel to one another on the rotating disks. Some people tend to be so "locked," that they forget to swivel their feet. Be sure your hands and feet shadow each other in parallel lines. During this movement, your fingers should also be moving from side to side.

7. Bend and straighten your elbows, lifting the index fingers up, then down, moving right to left, drawing an "infinity sign" ∞

8. Slowly widen your hands, unlocking your fingers, keeping your arms slightly concave and equal in length from your body's center. Allow your hips to pull through, following the same movement as your hands. By unlinking your fingers, you will begin to feel the fluid, drag of the arms.

As you do the Figure **8** motion, you will feel your hips pull your arms and feet into motion, as opposed to your hands initiating the movement. As one hip rises, the other one will fall. A constant flow of motion will take place due to the weight transfer, verticality, and horizontal movement. The key is to maintain your center while all this is taking place.

The only thing that is not moving is your head. Try to keep your eyes focused straight ahead, just as you would in a tennis match. Imagine a vertical line running directly through you from the top of your head down through the center of the 8board. Once you start to get the movement down, you'll realize that every part of your body is moving in a small figure **8**, including your hips, knees and shoulders. The ideal Figure 8 motion is initiated from the hips, resulting in the arms and feet always "catching up". Remember, there is no starting or stopping in the figure **8**. It is a continuous motion that the infinity sign symbolizes.

The Ultimate 3 Minute Workout

Get connected to your natural rhythm and *find your center* with the perfect **3** minute exercise that balances, stretches, and coordinates your entire body.

Make sure you are already familiar, comfortable and confident with your figure **8** form on the **8**board before trying the following exercise.

Many athletes might consider it impossible to greatly impact the body in just three minutes. However after practicing the **Ultimate 3-Minute Workout** on the **8**board, you will see just how effective it can be.

The following exercise will help you with everything from low back pain and rehabilitation, to virtually any sport, from golf to T'ai Chi.

The **8**Board Core-dination tips will help you with balance and coordination. The next three minutes should be one long continuous movement with no breaks or pauses between steps (or shall I say "swivels".) Repeat each move ten times.

1. Hands Linked In Front: Start in normal **8**Board stance, with your fingers interlaced and your index fingers pointing outward at a **45°** vertical. Begin to twist side to side at the hips, and slowly let your fingers follow. Repeat this movement ten times.

2. Hands Linked in Figure 8 Movement: Continue to twist side to side, now with your hands following the figure **8** path of motion. Repeat this ten times.

3. Hands Unlinked, Small Figure 8: Unlock your fingers. Let your hands widen, palms still facing one another, so that your entire body is doing the figure eight. Your hips should be the core of the movement. Repeat ten times.

4. Super Figure 8: Do the same movement as in Step **3**, only imagine a super wide figure eight – make big circles with your arms. Your arms should be slowing dragging behind, as if you were standing in neck-deep water. Repeat ten times.

5. Hands on Hips: Keep the fluid rotation as you slowly morph into placing your hands onto your hips. In this stance, you will feel the steady figure **8** formation in your center. By keeping your hands on your hips, the figure **8** movement becomes more of a challenge. During these ten repetitions, you will feel the stretch in your lower back.

6. Squatting: Gently lower your stance, so that you are slightly squatting. Keep your hands where you feel most balanced. Begin to feel the lifting and lowering of your hips. The verticality of this move will target your lower back and sides. During these ten repetitions, you will feel the working of your muscles in the quads and calves.

7. Hands Behind Back: Return to normal Figure **8** stance, with a slight bending at the knees. Slowly move your hands behind your back and clasp your wrists. Your elbows should be back, and your chest extended. As you continue to rotate ten times, lean back slightly so the muscles begin to work in your upper thighs.

8. Hands Behind Head: Unlink your hands from behind your back and link them behind your head. Imagine you are laying on a pillow with your hands folded behind your head. Your elbows should be pointed out and your chest extended. You will feel the stretch in your mid-to-upper back. To add variation, follow the figure **8** movement with your elbows and not just your hips. The entire time you are rotating, your eyes should be staring straight ahead and not at your feet. Repeat ten times.

9. Hands Above Head: Unlink your fingers and raise your hands to the sky. Your palms should be facing one-another and your fingers pointing upward. This will be a full body stretch as you continue to rotate ten times. Your entire body will bow out, as your hips glide around the corners of the figure **8**.

10. Arms Outstretched: In these ten rotations, lower your arms extended to the sides so that they are at shoulder level. This full-body exercise will be most effective in the rotator cuff, back, and hips. Here your elbows are pivotal, moving back and forth between concave and convex. You will feel a much bigger stretch in your lower back and shoulders. Depending on your preference, your arms can move in a small or a wide figure **8**. To make this move more challenging, hold your arms completely still while outstretched, working your shoulders, back and hips more aggressively.

11. Cool Down: In the final step, bend at the waist and allow your arms to dangle in front of you. Gently move from side to side, with your fingers dragging like a rake in the sand. Do this ten times, then stand up. As you step off the **8**Board, you will instantly feel connected to the Earth. Sudden movements will not feel so sudden. This simple **3**-Minute Exercise will allow you to flow into your day with balance and coordination.

Additional 8Board Variations

As these moves become more natural, you can explore the variations of the Figure **8**. Below is a list of figure **8** exercises that can be incorporated into your routine. Each one gives you another layer of coordination, balance, and flexibility.

1. Super Slow: Follow the same steps as the standard figure **8** movement, only move at a much slower pace. These slow-motion moves will allow you to perfect your form and focus on balance. This is also an excellent option for someone who is just learning how to use the **8Board**. At a slower pace you can feel your body working which will allow you to concentrate on form. By decreasing your speed, you can practice your tennis stroke or golf swing. This is a great way to get connected to your center.

2. Straps: Hold a strap or towel over your head, pulling the ends in opposite directions. You can also substitute a broomstick for a strap. Rotating in this stance allows you to be linear on top and non-linear down below. This will effectively stretch your pectorals, deltoids and back, which are usually difficult to isolate. During this dynamic stretching, you will become more coordinated as you continue to move.

3. Free Weights: This is a heavy-strength move and should only be utilized once you have mastered the standard figure **8** movement. Ideal for athletes in training, this move helps develop muscles and improves coordination, grace, and balance. With your elbows at your side, hold onto the weights as if there were an imaginary beach ball separating your hands. As one palm goes up, the other goes down and visa versa. You don't want to use much weight; one to five pounds at the most. You'll quickly realize that weight training using nonlinear motion is much more intense then simply pushing a weight in a linear motion. Cans of soup can be substituted for free weights.

4. Medicine Ball: Hold the medicine ball at waist level, unless your strength allows you to hold it at shoulder level. If you want to improve your golf swing, imitate the same moves with the medicine ball that you would on the course.

5. Spins: Continue to move in the figure **8** for ten rotations before launching off one foot and spinning entirely around on the other. Continue this process, switching back and forth between feet. This **360°** movement will tell you if you are balanced and will improve your momentum. The secret of this drill is to continue to turn facing one swivel before you lift up one foot. Remain aware of your vertical axis, when spinning. Also, be sure to keep your palms facing in, equidistant from your center.